MW00527504

Harlots and Heroines
The Midwives of the Messiah

by
Dr. Chuck F. Betters

In His Grip,
Chuck Betters

Harlots and Heroines: The Midwives of the Messiah

Copyright © 2009 by Dr. Chuck F. Betters

All rights reserved. Printed in the USA. No part of this book may be reproduced or transmitted in any form or by any means without written permission of the publisher.

New Heaven Publishing
P.O. Box 5711
Newark, DE 19714
(800) 655-2859

Cover design by D3 Graphic Design

ISBN 13: 978-0-9793859-7-1
ISBN 10: 0-9793859-7-0

Harlots and Heroines
The Midwives of the Messiah

Table of Contents

Acknowledgements

This project was a team effort. It could not have been completed without the dedication of my good friends Earle and Brenda Gould, who spent countless hours helping me to edit my sermons on this topic into book form.

The Godly women in my focus group provided invaluable input. Thank you for sacrificing time away from your families to help me with this book. Special thanks to Barbie Betters, my niece, and to Elena Brenner, Karen Dekker, Christine Funston Lewis, Michal Jackson, and Bev Lum, all of whom invested significant effort in the editing process.

The Session of the Glasgow Reformed Presbyterian Church, where I have served since 1986 as the Senior Pastor, has greatly encouraged me in my preaching, teaching and writing. Thank you, my brothers, for your support.

To the wonderful women at Glasgow Church who have encouraged and supported me in this project, please know that this pastor is extremely blessed to serve alongside of you in Kingdom-building.

Finally, my wife Sharon and I have been blessed with three special women, the spiritual Midwives of our fourteen grandchildren—our daughter, Heidi Nequist, and our two daughters-in-law, Melanie Betters and Laura Betters. Thank you for modeling Christ to your children. It makes our hearts sing with joy unspeakable.

Dedication

This book is dedicated to the two Midwives in my life–my mother, Florence Betters, who raised me as a boy, and my wife of 40 years, Sharon Watts Betters, who raised me as a man.

Preface

On July 6, 1993, my family experienced the nightmare of the sudden and tragic death of our 16 year-old son, Mark. I verbalized my agony of soul this way: "Lord, I thought you were my father–my dad. I do not understand this. I too am a dad. I would never treat my kids this way. Why are you treating me like this? Why was this necessary?"

I have seen tragedy, horrific pain and death touch the lives of more precious people than I can bear to recall. I have stood beside fresh graves and tried to come up with just the right words on God's behalf to dry even one of the tears streaming down the faces of devastated children and spouses. I have peered through their hollow eyes and heard the cry of their souls, "Why was this necessary?" I do not have enough pages in this book to give you a satisfactory answer to that question, nor could I if I did. All the books in the world cannot address that question, for there are some wounds only heaven can heal. By sin, death entered the world as an ugly, vicious and relentless enemy. It is only because of a baby born in Bethlehem two thousand years ago that this grotesque enemy has been defeated.

I do not hesitate for a moment to identify with my five sisters in this book. When I held my son's body in my arms that soul-scorching night in the hospital, my heart cried out, "Lord, You have got to show me that everything I have ever believed about You is true because right now, I do not believe any of it." As I write these words years later, I still do not know all of the answers. These years of God-empowered

Grace to trust and believe Him have reassured my soul with the promise that our God is sovereign and that He can be trusted. That is what this book is all about– a sovereign God Who can be trusted!

A record of the genealogy of Jesus Christ the son of David, the son of Abraham: Abraham was the father of Isaac, Isaac the father of Jacob, Jacob the father of Judah and his brothers, Judah the father of Perez and Zerah, ***whose mother was Tamar,*** *Perez the father of Hezron, Hezron the father of Ram, Ram the father of Amminadab, Amminadab the father of Nahshon, Nahshon the father of Salmon, Salmon the father of Boaz,* ***whose mother was Rahab****, Boaz the father of Obed,* ***whose mother was Ruth****, Obed the father of Jesse, and Jesse the father of King David. David was the father of Solomon,* ***whose mother had been Uriah's wife****, Solomon the father of Rehoboam, Rehoboam the father of Abijah, Abijah the father of Asa, Asa the father of Jehoshaphat, Jehoshaphat the father of Jehoram, Jehoram the father of Uzziah, Uzziah the father of Jotham, Jotham the father of Ahaz, Ahaz the father of Hezekiah, Hezekiah the father of Manasseh, Manasseh the father of Amon, Amon the father of Josiah, and Josiah the father of Jeconiah and his brothers at the time of the exile to Babylon. After the exile to Babylon: Jeconiah was the father of Shealtiel, Shealtiel the father of Zerubbabel, Zerubbabel the father of Abiud, Abiud the father of Eliakim, Eliakim the father of Azor, Azor the father of Zadok, Zadok the father of Akim, Akim the father of Eliud, Eliud the father of Eleazar, Eleazar the father of Matthan, Matthan the father of Jacob, and Jacob the father of Joseph,* **the husband of Mary***, of whom was born Jesus, who is called Christ. Thus there were fourteen generations in all from Abraham to David, fourteen from David to the exile to Babylon, and fourteen from the exile to the Christ.* (Matthew 1:1-17; emphasis added)

Introduction

A wounded widow...a professional prostitute...an indomitable immigrant...a bathing beauty...a terrified teenager. What do these five women have in common? They were all an integral part of the plan God made in eternity past to come to this earth as a man. The theological term for that event is the *Incarnation*. These women were God's conduits of love and the chosen instruments of the Incarnation who brought "Joy to the World." Their chorus of pain, loss and eventual redemption gave voice to the Angelic Host who brought the very first Christmas Carol to the hills outside of Bethlehem. God condescended in Grace to use these five mangled masses of frightened and scarred humanity to become the Midwives of the Messiah!

Where in the Bible do we automatically go to read about the beauty and the inspiration of the birth of the Messiah, that first Christmas? The New Testament of course. Christmas started there, right? We read in the Gospels of Matthew and Luke the fascinating account of a young, expectant couple on an exhausting journey along the rocky road to Bethlehem. The Gospel accounts describe crowded streets and a hotel with no vacancies; a cold, smelly stable; shepherds minding their sheep in the dark of night in nearby fields and, of course, the star-gazing Magi.

Now, think for a moment about these familiar scenes–the cast of characters is composed exclusively of men, with the exception of the very young mother-to-be, Mary, and her cousin, Elizabeth. As we will soon discover, however, Mary—

as central as she is in the telling of the traditional Christmas story—was not alone. She was but one of several prominent women we find on the long trail of tears that lead us to that joyous night in Bethlehem. But "the greatest story ever told" did not have its beginning in Bethlehem. Mary, in her obedience to the promptings of God's Holy Spirit, stood in the good–or at least curious—company of several other women who went before her. Let me introduce you to five *Harlots and Heroines—The Midwives of the Messiah.*

~ ~ ~ ~

Let us begin with some insight on the religious and cultural setting in which the Incarnation story took shape. The valuable role women have played in major history-making events and the credit they are given might not be considered unusual in our modern world, but the inclusion of women certainly was regarded with suspicion among many first century Jews. Had the story originated at the hands of this male-dominated society alone, the hope of a coming Messiah would likely not have included the indispensible contribution of women. But the Incarnation of the Messiah and all of the preceding history that made it possible originated in the heart and mind of God, not by the whims of man.

One aspect we must truly understand and take the time to investigate, as we consider the bigger picture behind the Incarnation story, is the genealogy of Jesus. The very special women we want to meet are found here.

Matthew chapter 1 and Luke chapter 3 trace the human family tree of Jesus. To some, these may arguably be two of the most boring chapters in the Bible. Yet, as with all Scripture, God put them there for a reason. The chapters are filled with the names of people whom many of us are only vaguely familiar with, the possible exceptions being the more recognizable names like Abraham, Isaac, Jacob, and David. Here in the Scriptures (King James Version) we find those famous "begats"—so and so begat so and so who begat so and so through seemingly endless generations, culminating in due time with the birth of Jesus Christ. Tedious reading to say the least, yet profitable, as we are about to see.

The New Testament genealogy was not unique in the time frame in which it was written and for its diligent recording of a person's detailed ancestry. If you were a Roman citizen in those days, much emphasis was placed on your family genealogy. Your class status in society was largely dependent upon your pedigree through a socially and racially acceptable lineage. One could actually be accepted in the lofty circles of royalty if their family history and financial status met certain arbitrary and elitist standards. Similarly, in Greek culture, the bloodline defined who you were as a family and thus dictated your status in society. Written genealogies, carefully researched and documented, were a prized possession for any person of means in that era.

In Jewish culture, the treatment of a genealogy differed from that of other people groups in that the foretold Messiah played a central part in the history, religion, contemporary worldview and concept of the future for every serious Jew. The Rabbis knew that it was religiously critical that the family tree of the coming Messiah contained three core tap roots: First, the Messiah *must* have His origins in Abraham, Isaac and Jacob, the fathers of the Covenant. Second, the Messiah *must* find His identity in another offspring of Abraham, namely, the tribe of Judah. Third, the Messiah *must* trace His roots through the greatest of all Old Testament kings, King David. If a religious Jew wished to trace his own historical family roots, King David was as far back as he would really need to go to establish his social and religious authenticity. Proven roots that traced back to Abraham, Judah, and David guaranteed unassailable credentials among the chosen people of God's Covenant.

Matthew wrote his Gospel with a Jewish target audience in mind. He traced the genealogy of Jesus through his legal father, Joseph, in order to validate Jesus as the King of the Jews, Israel's Messiah and legal heir to the throne of David. Luke, on the other hand, wrote his Gospel to a Greek audience who were not as concerned about fulfillment of Jewish prophecy in Jesus' royal bloodline. Luke's purpose was to identify

Jesus as the "*Son of God*"—a Gentile term—to a society that worshipped many gods. Thus, His lineage was traced through His mother, Mary, all the way back to Adam.

The Apostle John states the purpose in writing his Gospel this way: *But these are written that you may believe that Jesus is the Christ, the son of God, and that by believing you may have life in his name* (John 20:31). Even though John does not include the genealogy of Jesus, he told us that he was writing with two audiences in mind. When he used the term, *the Christ,* he carefully chose a word with which a Jewish audience would readily identify. And when he used the term *Son of God,* Gentiles would more readily take notice. Our Messiah, Jesus, the Son of God, came for a purpose–to secure salvation for His people without regard for race, gender or nationality. Christ's genealogy in the Gospels appropriately reflects that inclusiveness.

Here is where we are introduced to what some ancients would consider, at best, a controversial level of inclusiveness–the first appearance of a *woman* in the bloodline of the Messiah. Enter Tamar...

In the story of Tamar, a wounded widow and the first of the Midwives of the Messiah, we will snap a picture of God's marvelous Grace and Mercy. In spite of her great deception, God used her pain to form a critical link in the coming of our Messiah, the Lord Jesus Christ. Truly our God can bring beauty out of ashes.

Chapter One: Tamar

A record of the genealogy of Jesus Christ the son of David, the son of Abraham: Abraham was the father of Isaac, Isaac the father of Jacob, Jacob the father of Judah and his brothers, Judah the father of Perez and Zerah, whose mother was Tamar... (Matthew 1:1-3a; emphasis added)

Five women played a key role in the shaping of the Incarnation story. In the patriarchal society of that day, acknowledging any female—let alone five—in a Jewish genealogy was unusual, if not downright frowned upon...but they are there.

The first of these five women appears in Genesis 38. Her name was Tamar. God placed her there for a very special reason. Lessons are to be learned from this strategic placement on the bumpy road to Bethlehem. Consider this:

At that time, Judah left his brothers and went down to stay with a man of Adullam named Hirah. There Judah met the daughter of a Canaanite man named Shua. He married her and lay with her; she became pregnant and gave birth to a son, who was named Er. She conceived again and gave birth to a son named Onan. She gave birth to still another son and named him Shelah. It was at Kezib that she gave birth to him. (Genesis 38:1-5)

Notice the first three words in verse 1, At that time. In all likelihood, the period referred to occurred when Judah was a young man. He had just endured a traumatic and notorious episode in his life when he brazenly conspired with his brothers to sell Joseph, their younger brother and favorite of their father, Jacob, into slavery. On the heels of this grotesque sin, Judah parted company with his sibling conspirators. We can assume that shame, guilt, and fear over what he had done motivated him to set out for Adullam, home to the king of the Canaanites, the avowed enemy of Israel.

Shockingly, Judah was about to ingratiate himself with the royal household of the Canaanites. He seemed to have established a track record of one disastrous moral decision after another. He also foolishly formed a close relationship with a man named Hirah, a resident of Adullam. With his new-found friend, Judah was well on his way to the complete abandonment of all Godly protection, authority and instruction–making him easy prey for the Tempter.

This is the same Judah who, through his own descendants, became the father of the "line of Judah" by which the Messiah would come—a set of credentials that we would expect him to have handled much more responsibly. After all, any self-proclaimed messiah in Israel who could not trace his ancestry back to the line of Judah would certainly have been identified as an imposter. Remember, the Messiah must come from the tribe of Judah. The tribe's namesake was certainly getting off to a disappointing start.

The saga continued as Judah met a young woman, the daughter of Shua. Although her own name is not given, her family name, Shua, has a double meaning in the Hebrew language, denoting either, "wealth and riches" or, in stark contrast, "a cry for help."[1] Judah dwelt in a hostile, foreign land and was about to marry into a prominent, wealthy, non-Jewish family. Yet, one can almost hear his "cry for help" as he was about to self-destruct.

Young Judah and the girl we'll call by her family name, Shua, foolishly married and soon reaped the consequences of their immaturity. Young Shua soon bore three sons; Judah named the first son, Er. The double meaning of his name, "the watcher" or "the evil one," gives us some warning as to the nature of his character in later life. Shua named the second son Onan, or "strength." Shua was also the one who named their third son, Shelah. Curious–since it was customary for the father to name his children, one might inquire as to where Judah was during the birth and naming process of his last two sons? Judah may have been an absentee dad who was, at least emotionally, if not physically, disengaged from his family. Er, in keeping with the interpretation of his name, went on to live a lifestyle of intense immorality. We could justifiably call him a "chip off the old block." Er may have strongly influenced Shua in the naming of their second son, "strength." After dealing with a sinful, immature husband and a rebellious, evil "number one son," we can easily imagine Shua crying out, "Lord, give me strength!"

Interestingly, the third son was given the name, Shelah, meaning "pray for peace." The sequence of names gives us a portrait of a family in turmoil. Here we have a mother whose husband and sons did not walk with God. Judah was either not aware of, or chose to disregard, his critical role in a family lineage that would lead to the coming of the Messiah. Yet, for His own good purposes, God chose in Grace to use Judah as part of His ordained Messianic line.

Judah arranged the marriage of his first son, Er, to a woman named Tamar, a Canaanite from Adullam who was likely very young at the time. Her name means "date tree" or "palm tree," and that too would play out in this drama. We are not given much detail about Er as a person other than that he managed, through some unspecified sinful behavior, to seriously provoke God's displeasure: *Judah got a wife for Er, his firstborn, and her name was Tamar. But Er, Judah's firstborn, was wicked in the Lord's sight; so the Lord put him to death* (Genesis 38:6-7).

Some scholars have suggested that the nature of the word "wicked" indicates Er's wrongdoing was marital or sexual in nature, that his sin affected and infected his marriage relationship and brought disgrace upon him and his entire family line. The effect of the sin was self-polluting, perhaps a sexually transmitted disease. Whatever it was, the sin was grotesque in the sight of God. We are not told exactly how Er was killed, but the literal Hebrew translation is—*the Lord caused him to die*. God delivered him over to the consequences of his sin, leading directly to his sudden, unexpected demise.

Tamar was now left as a young and childless widow. Her life story was about to take on an interesting twist:

Then Judah said to Onan, "Lie with your brother's wife and fulfill your duty to her as a brother-in-law to produce offspring for your brother." But Onan knew that the offspring would not be his; so whenever he lay with his brother's wife, he spilled his semen on the ground to keep from producing offspring for his brother. (Genesis 38:8-9)

Onan's behavior was directly related to his knowledge of the law of the Levirate found in Deuteronomy 25. Levirate law was intended to protect young women who became widows at an early age, most often due to her husband's death in battle. The deceased husband's brother was to assume the marital relationship with the woman, even to the extent of producing children with her. Thus, the deceased husband's lineage would continue uninterrupted *so that his name will not be blotted out from Israel* (Deuteronomy 25:6b). Levirate marriage meant that such children became the rightful heirs to the *deceased* husband's property and would carry on *his* name. Thus, Onan made a willful decision to violate Jewish law and terminate his brother's family name. So God took drastic measures with him as well:

What he [Onan] did was wicked in the Lord's sight; so he put him to death also (Genesis 38:10).

Evidence shows that, in spite of their moral failings, God had a very special plan for the line of Judah that tragically involved the deaths of two wicked men within the family. Take careful notice that, if Onan had paid as much attention to preserving his brother's heritage as he did with lining his own pockets, he would have been blessed with the inexpressible privilege of carrying forth the lineage of the coming Anointed One. Onan was not about to have any children by Tamar. He knew that all of the property rights of Tamar's dead husband would have devolved to her and her offspring, which meant that any inheritance he anticipated from Judah would be reduced. Thus, he chose material possessions over eternal spiritual blessings. We see God's continuing displeasure with, and His willingness to make an example of, any attempts to disrupt His ordained Messianic birth line.

In Genesis 38:10 we read, *What he did was wicked in the Lord's sight; so he put him to death also*. The word for "Lord" in this verse is the word Yahweh, the name for God that distinguishes Him as the God of the Covenant. This is Yahweh, the "Great I Am," Who promised to build a family extending from Abraham through Isaac, through Jacob, through Moses and David, and through the prophets, culminating in the coming of Jesus, our Savior and Messiah. That name, Yahweh, is critical to understanding why God ended the lives of Judah's two sons. At stake was the promise of a Redeemer through the line of Judah (see Genesis 12:1-3 and the remarkable drama of Genesis 15), a Redeemer Who would save His people from their sins. The Redeemer is Yahweh, the God of the Covenant. These two sons were blinded from seeing God's perspective because of their sinfulness. It cost them their lives.

We can now only imagine what Judah may have been thinking after two of his sons—who had married the same woman—ended up dead. Tamar may have been viewed as a "black widow," someone a potential husband would have definitely wanted to avoid. In fact, there was an ancient superstition prevalent in Judah's day, originating in the apocryphal book of Tobit, in which a woman who lost two husbands in a row was thereafter to be treated by everyone as cursed. Judah may have bought into such superstition. As a father, he surely had a natural fear for the safety of his youngest son, Shelah, who was just a child at the time.

Out of what appeared to be a sincere fear of God, we see in Genesis 38:11 that Judah decided to exercise his absolute right as father-in-law over Tamar. She was still his legal daughter-in-law and would remain so until her death. Judah mandated that she must live as a widow, lonely and forsaken in her own father's house, and Judah would financially provide for her in return. He cruelly insisted that she live like this until his third son, Shelah, became an adult. By making such a decision, Judah's family line would continue through the offspring of Shelah and Tamar, although Judah, indeed, harbored fears that *He [Shelah] may die too, just like his brothers* (Genesis 38:12).

We can sense Judah's strong reluctance to ever follow through with his promise to Tamar. He was not about to risk Shelah's life with this woman. So, in his hypocrisy, Judah attempted to maintain the appearance of complying with Jewish law and retain some semblance of public respect while effectively living a lie and ruining this young widow's life.

Having little regard for his extended legacy, Judah acted in a way that was consistent with his youth and immaturity. He had only recently sold his brother into slavery, he was an irresponsible dad, and he had raised two disobedient sons who ended up dead. His family was dysfunctional at best. This Biblical soap opera continued as the scene shifted to the land of Canaan sometime later....

After a long time Judah's wife, the daughter of Shua, died. When Judah had recovered from his grief, he went up to Timnah, to the men who were shearing his sheep, and his friend Hirah the Adullamite went with him. (Genesis 38:12)

In Jewish tradition, the grieving period could last up to two years. After Judah's grief period ended, Hirah the Adullamite, his bad-influence Canaanite friend, was still hanging around. The two of them went to Timnah to take part in the sheep-shearing festival, a Mardi Gras-like atmosphere that was almost exclusively dedicated to the practice of all kinds of sexual entertainments and perversions. The party was given in honor of the goddess Astarte. This fact would very likely not have been a surprise to Judah since, by this time, his moral guard appeared to have completely collapsed. He went with the full expectation of enjoying himself with the "sacred" prostitutes who were an integral part of this idolatrous celebration.

Judah's interests had turned completely inward. After the death of two sons and his wife, he may very well have concluded that he was entitled to his own pity party and some long overdue self-indulgence. We can reasonably imagine that his thinking went something like this: "It's been a long time since I've had an intimate relationship with a woman. It's time to start looking out for number one. I have had so much tragedy in my life. Now, it's time for me to pay some attention to me." So he and his old friend Hirah took off on this "business trip" to Canaan. Little did he know what awaited him just down the road.

When Tamar was told, "Your father-in-law is on his way to Timnah to shear his sheep," she took off her widow's clothes, covered herself with a veil to disguise herself, and then sat down at the entrance to Enaim, which is on the road to Timnah. For she saw that, though Shelah had now grown up, she had not been given to him as his wife. When Judah saw her, he thought she was a prostitute, for she had covered her face. Not realizing that she was his daughter-in-law, he went over to her by the roadside and said, "Come now, let me sleep with you."

"And what will you give me to sleep with you?" she asked.

"I'll send you a young goat from my flock," he said.

"Will you give me something as a pledge until you send it?" she asked.

He said, "What pledge should I give you?"

"Your seal and its cord, and the staff in your hand," she answered. So he gave them to her and slept with her, and she became pregnant by him. After she left, she took off her veil and put on her widow's clothes again.

Meanwhile Judah sent the young goat by his friend the Adullamite in order to get his pledge back from the woman, but he did not find her. (Genesis 38:13-20)

Tamar remained loyal to Judah's promise and continued for many years to wear the clothes of a grieving widow. However, when she was informed that Judah was on his way to the city where she was living, she decided that she had waited long enough. She surprisingly resorted to a great deception of her own in order to continue the family line. Posing as a veiled prostitute, she tricked Judah into sleeping with her. Judah had already realized that he had left his "checkbook" and "credit cards" at home. So, he promised payment for her affections by leaving with her, as surety, his signet ring, cord, and staff, all very valuable items of personal identification in those days.

Upon returning home, Judah sent the promised payment, a young goat, to Tamar by way of his friend, Hirah. He did so in the full expectation that he would receive back his valuable ring, cord and staff and that no one would be the wiser. But things took a dramatic turn:

He [Hirah] asked the men who lived there, "Where is the shrine prostitute who was beside the road at Enaim?" "There hasn't been any shrine prostitute here," they said. So he went back to Judah and said, "I didn't find her. Besides, the men who lived there said, 'There hasn't been any shrine prostitute here.'" Then Judah said, "Let her keep what she has, or we will become a laughing-stock. After all, I did send her this young goat, but you didn't find her." (Genesis 38:21-23)

In this instance, we catch an insightful glimpse into Judah's heart. His greater concern was for his own reputation and not for his involvement with a prostitute or his payment obligation to her. He knew that any diligent search for this woman would expose what he had done–that he, as a Jew, bound by the law not to engage in these kinds of relationships, was having a sexual tryst with a woman he thought was a Canaanite temple prostitute. Tragically, up until then, there was no apparent shame or repentance for his sin. Judah had entered a seemingly terminal, downward moral spiral.

He left town and, because of his poor decisions and the personal ruin that they brought upon him, he eventually ended up a lonely, desperate old man. But his life's bumpy ride was not over quite yet:

About three months later Judah was told, "Your daughter-in-law Tamar is guilty of prostitution, and as a result she is now pregnant."

Judah said, "Bring her out and have her burned to death!"

As she was being brought out, she sent a message to her father-in-law. "I am pregnant by the man who owns these," she said. And she added, "See if you recognize whose seal and cord and staff these are."

Judah recognized them and said, "She is more righteous than I, since I wouldn't give her to my son Shelah." And he did not sleep with her again. (Genesis 38:24-26)

This is a curious passage indeed, not only for Judah's hypocrisy and cruelty toward his own daughter-in-law, but also in his humbly commending Tamar for being more righteous than he in the way that this whole episode panned out. The act of deception on Tamar's part raises some interesting questions as well. Was she right or wrong in prostituting herself and committing this act of incest with her father-in-law? On one side of the argument, she engaged in prostitution and incest. These behaviors cannot be justified anywhere in Scripture. Any sensible judgment would have to immediately condemn Tamar as being morally wrong in God's sight. On the other hand, as we examine her motivation for doing what she did (although she could have done it a different way), we have to acknowledge her deep concern that the lines of Judah and her dead husband were at stake. In her weakness and in spite of her sin, she was more committed to preserving Judah's birth line than was Judah. I am sure Messianic hope was not her primary motivation. Had she not acted however, the lineage of the Messiah would have been endangered since only Shelah was left. Since God had already killed his two older brothers, there certainly was no guarantee Shelah would live long enough to father any offspring, nor was there any guarantee Judah would ever give Shelah to Tamar.

Judah realized that he had driven Tamar to take drastic measures to preserve the bloodline according to the law, which is why he had to confess, *She is more righteous than I am* (Genesis 38:26). Could this instant turn-about in attitude be an early hint of sincere repentance developing in Judah's heart? Perhaps!

All Bible stories are real-life dramas. They were written that we might be instructed in the ways of our God Who stooped in Grace to the level of sinful man. God did so while not compromising His Righteousness and sovereignty. The story of Judah and Tamar is not any different morally from God's plan and purpose coming to fruition through such evil events as the selling of Joseph into slavery, David's adulterous affair with Bathsheba and his resultant murder of her husband Uriah, or Peter's denial of Christ, to name only a few. The Scriptures do not teach that two wrongs can ever make a right. In fact, painful consequences and devastation followed these individuals. Their offences are described in graphic detail in the Bible to serve as dire warnings to subsequent generations that God will never turn a blind eye to sin, whatever the extenuating circumstances. Through the life stories of these flawed men and women we are to understand this truth—what man meant for evil, God meant for good in order to accomplish His sovereign purpose (Genesis 50:20). We are left to bow in humble gratitude that He still works all things together for good in this same way for us.

It was time for Tamar to give birth:

When the time came for her to give birth, there were twin boys in her womb. As she was giving birth, one of them put out his hand; so the mid-wife took a scarlet thread and tied it on his wrist and said, "This one came out first." But when he drew back his hand, his brother came out, and she said, "So this is how you have broken out!" And he was named Perez. Then his brother, who had the scarlet thread on his wrist, came out and he was given the name Zerah. (Genesis 38:27-30)

Nothing is written in Scripture without a reason. The name Perez means "the breech" or "break out," and Zerah means, "splendor" or "brightness." These names have great significance in the context of the story. Out of Tamar's horrible and painful ordeal, in which she suffered great heartache and likely abuse at the hands of her husband, Er, something amazing happened. Just as weary travelers found shade and relief from the hot sun under the palm tree, she too, as her name indicates (palm tree or date tree) would find shade and relief from the blazing sun of abuse under the palm tree of God's amazing love and watchfulness over her.

Let's take a look at that "most boring chapter" in the Bible....

A record of the genealogy of Jesus Christ the son of David, the son of Abraham: Abraham was the father of Isaac, Isaac the father of Jacob, Jacob the father of Judah and his brothers, Judah the father of Perez and Zerah, whose mother was Tamar... (Matthew 1:1-3a)

There she was—an eternal, bona fide member of Jesus' earthly family tree. For the writers of the Old Testament to place a woman's name in the Messianic genealogy—especially this woman, after what she did—suggests she was indeed "more righteous" than Judah, at least by comparison, in this particular episode in their lives.

The passage continues:

...Perez the father of Hezron, Hezron the father of Ram, Ram the father of Amminadab, Amminadab the father of Nahshon, Nahshon the father of Salmon, Salmon the father of Boaz, whose mother was Rahab, Boaz the father of Obed, whose mother was Ruth, Obed the father of Jesse, and Jesse the father of King David. David was the father of Solomon, whose mother had been Uriah's wife ... (Matthew 1:3b-6)

Here are the bookends: On the one end, Abraham; on the other, David; and in the middle, Judah. The births of Perez and Zerah were Judah's link in the Messianic lineage. Because of God's Grace and, in spite of Judah's hypocrisy and Tamar's deception, the lineage of Judah continued. Thus, Tamar's name appears in the genealogy of Jesus. She was our first Midwife of the Messiah.

Well, this is all very interesting, but not very different from a modern drama-filled TV soap opera. Tamar's story could almost pass for another gripping episode of *All My Children*, *General Hospital*, or the eye-catching headlines of the supermarket tabloids we are bombarded with on a daily basis...*except* that the Biblical episode is true and has eternal implications. Unlike the soaps, Tamar did not step onto the pages of the Old Testament as a source of entertainment or sensationalism. She formed an integral element in the long, scarlet thread of tears that weaved its way from Eden to Bethlehem. Our God kept His eternal promise of redemption and became our Messiah, in spite of the seemingly impossible dilemmas of sinful men and women. Yet, the One Who saves His people from their sins calls them—and us—*friend*. Pure Grace! Another block was laid on the historic foundation that would shape and give deeper significance to the meaning of the Incarnation.

Tamar's story and its affirmation in Matthew chapter 1 demonstrate the infallibility and trustworthiness of all Scripture, the continuity and mutual validation of the Old and New Testaments, and the reliability of the many prophecies pointing to the coming of Christ. A false or contrived genealogy could have easily been fabricated to exclude a female figure in order to present a more socially acceptable "messiah story" and placate certain sensitivities. That is not how our God works. What a stark contrast to the man-made cults of today who find it necessary to fabricate idealistic and suspiciously perfect biographies of their spiritual leaders and false "messiahs" in order to attract and mesmerize the desperate and the uninformed. The Bible tells it like it is—pimples, warts and all, even if it makes the characters look like anything but heroic. There is no cover-up, no cosmetic editing and no salesmanship or white-washing of the facts.

Let us review several important ways in which the story of Tamar prepares our hearts to understand the great significance of the Incarnation and lend insight into the *path of pain* and Grace that brought the God of the universe to a manger in Bethlehem:

The story of Tamar reminds us of God's preeminence and marvelous Grace in the face of great moral depravity. Jesus came to identify with, and embrace as His family, sinful people like you and me. In clear view for all to see in Jesus' family line are prophets, kings, the rich and the poor, listed alongside of cheats, prostitutes, liars and imposters. Yet, through this "rogue's gallery" of seriously flawed characters and shocking events, His love and forbearance shine majestically through. His sovereignty, even over the most depraved acts of men, is a clear testimony to the extent to which He will go to accomplish His purposes. We are utterly unworthy of a God who condescended to become a man and provide such a rich salvation to undeserving sinners. After all, this is the meaning of Grace...*For it is by grace you have been saved, through faith–and this not from yourselves, it is the gift of God—not by works, so that no one can boast* (Ephesians 2:8-9).

The story of Tamar forms a critical link in the ongoing drama of Biblical Prophecy. God in Christ could have simply chosen to appear on earth as a full-grown man. Instead, He chose to unerringly fulfill what He told Satan He was going to do—all the way back in the Garden of Eden. What did God say to the serpent? *The Seed of the Woman will crush your head!* (Genesis 3:15; emphasis added). In other words, God promised to crush Satan's head through the seed of a woman, a human being. No other means would have afforded the Messiah the credentials He needed to identify with sinners and qualify as our sin-substitute. All of Old Testament history is "His Story," the story of the seed-of-the-woman's struggle against the unrelenting Powers of Darkness. Satan desperately sought to destroy the woman's seed. He reasoned that, in so doing, he would terminate the coming of any Messiah. I can imagine Satan saying, "Judah's heart is hardened. He is saturated in grief. He will never give up his baby boy Shelah to Tamar. With two boys already dead, it is only a matter of time before Shelah joins his brothers in the grave. And with Tamar locked up in her home, she will not be having any babies by Judah's line. There will be no offspring to carry on the line of Judah and that means there will be no Messiah. I WIN!" WRONG!

The story of Tamar is a living example of how God has chosen to accomplish His Eternal Covenant of Redemption through frail and at times unwitting humanity. Once God had irreversibly declared His eternal Covenant of Grace, the Messiah could not come from any of the twelve tribes of Israel, save Judah. Judah's line was at best in danger of obliteration. Due to their evil, God killed Judah's two oldest sons. Only the boy Shelah remained. Judah was not about to give him up. No problem—enter Tamar. No wonder she holds a rightful and necessary place in the genealogy. What a "family" she had to call her own. The four eldest sons of Jacob (Judah's father) were horribly immoral men. Reuben and Judah had committed incest while Simeon and Levi were murderers. Nonetheless, God saw fit to bring about the priesthood out of Levi's line and the Messiah out of Judah's line via Tamar. How can we miss Grace in this exciting and unpredictable story? The granting of God's favor has absolutely nothing to do with how good or deserving man is. *The Eternal Covenant of Redemption* was conceived in the Council of the Trinity in eternity-past, and it was there that His Elect were named before any could claim merit of their own. In that same Council, God ordained that an otherwise obscure woman named Tamar would become a perfectly-fitting puzzle piece in God's plan to come as our Messiah.

What should the story of Tamar and Judah mean to us? *We* are Judah and Tamar with the same sinful propensities as they had. We are morally depraved people who, apart from God's intervening Grace, are capable of doing the same things they did and worse. However, God has an eternal plan and purpose wherein He extends that same marvelous redemption to us today. One by one, He calls us by name. He numbers the hairs on our heads. He knows us intimately and chose us before the foundation of the world and fashioned us in our mother's womb.

Upon His birth, Jesus stormed the very gates of hell and they have not stopped shaking and crumbling to this day. Despite their concerted efforts in opposition, the forces of evil stood in awe as they witnessed ancient prophecy come to pass through the miraculous birth of an infant in a manger. God's words resonated ominously in Satan's ears that night: *The Seed of the Woman will crush your head!*

A war began, unlike any the universe had ever seen. A myriad of battles raged for thousands of years leading up to the Messiah Who would come from a borrowed womb. The war intensified as Jesus, Who lived in one borrowed home after another, walked among the people preaching the good news, healing the sick, and raising the dead. The war thundered on a hill outside of Jerusalem called Golgotha as the Son of God willingly laid down His life on a borrowed cross. The victory was won as a two-ton stone that sealed a borrowed grave was blown out of its track with a heavenly heat, not in order to let Jesus out, but to let the world in to see that *He is not here; he has risen, just as he said* (Matthew 28:6). To this day, and until Christ returns, this defeated but persistent enemy seeks to reverse history, blot out belief in the Incarnation and destroy Christ's Church.

Believers can hold to an eternal Hope emanating from a stable in Bethlehem and take great comfort in knowing that Satan's defeat at the Cross is permanent. There is beauty and blessed assurance in what you and I as Christians believe—that our sovereign God is moving purposely through history. Personal circumstances or current world events ought not to threaten our peace and joy in Him. If God can choreograph every footstep of a weary couple on the lonely road to Bethlehem, and if He can redeem the deceptive behavior of Tamar and the moral depravity of Judah, He will preserve His Church and remain faithful to all who have put their trust in Him.

Tamar became one piece of a fascinating "puzzle." A virgin birth? A helpless baby in a manger? Astrologers? Kings from the East following a star for two years? Shepherds, outcasts of society serenaded by angels? Nonsense! Or is it? The Incarnation is anything but predictable and boring. One would be hard-pressed today to imagine how the birth of Perez and Zerah, and the actions of a woman like Tamar, could possibly fit into such a complex series of events. But as

He did in times past, God still accomplishes His purposes through unpredictable means and the use of unlikely, flawed human beings. He still delights in surprising us.

The story of Tamar reflects and amplifies the love of God. As with the first Christmas, we see in Tamar's story how God repeatedly chooses the "foolish" things of this world, such as what cynics might say is the "tabloid" genealogy of an infant born in a dirty stable, to redeem our sins and bear our sorrow. He is not ashamed of us and chooses in pure love to forget our sinful past when we repent and turn to Him no matter what we've done, no matter how immoral we have become and no matter how low we have stooped. Our God is not ashamed to put His arms around us and call us His sons and daughters. Just as He loved Judah, Tamar, Perez and Zerah in spite of one huge moral blunder after another, and just as He redeemed their faults to bring about the birth of the Savior, He embraces us and says, *"I have loved you with an everlasting love."* His love is the essence of the Incarnation for all who are in Christ and the hope of the Christmas story for all who still seek Him.

The story of Tamar underscores the pain mingled with joy that characterized the first Christmas. The first Christmas was not about jingle bells, snowmen or Santa Claus. Certainly, there was great joy as the shepherds witnessed a myriad of angels singing of God's glory and His offer of peace for His people. However, the pain of the first Christmas could be seen everywhere.[2] The *real* first Christmas was also filled with heartache and death in Ramah after Herod ordered the mass execution of every male child two years-old or younger. In a setting wrought with sorrow and fear, Joseph and Mary ran for their own lives and the life of their child.

Tamar's story in Genesis 38 was a precursor to the familiar Christmas story. A drama played out involving the joyful birth of two other babies whose manner of arrival gave a deeper perspective on the meaning of Christmas. *When Zerah's hand reached out, the midwife wrapped a scarlet thread around it* (Genesis 38:28). The hand quickly retracted, and the twin brother, Perez, instead became the first born.

The symbolism in these boys' names as well as their birth sequence is notable. The breech, Perez's "breaking out" ahead of Zerah, symbolized Christ at the Cross. The scarlet splendor, the thread around the wrist, symbolized the Church and our blood-bought salvation purchased at Calvary through great love and at a great price. *We* are the ones with the scarlet thread around our wrists, and Jesus alone has the power to breech death and hell on our behalf. He had to go ahead of us in order that we might wear the scarlet thread—the free gift of eternal life.

Jesus had to face the Cross and unimaginable pain and sacrifice *after* He was born. Similarly, the story of Tamar generations before painted a portrait of this joy mingled with pain in the birth of her twin babies, but in the context of a life filled with tragedy and sacrifice. Both Tamar's story and the birth of Jesus are a glorious blending of pain and joy. Through the breech—that is, through Perez who was a foreshadowing of Christ to come—and the joy and splendor of the Church signified by Zerah and the scarlet thread, our salvation was brought forth. That is why the genealogy includes not only Perez but also of Zerah. The Incarnation story would be incomplete if the account of Tamar's tragic life did not include both of the boys she bore. The twins were inseparable as they unwittingly gazed down through heaven's telescope to another baby lying peacefully in a manger. The pain and splendor they represent, and the trail of sorrows of which they were an integral part, are an appropriate foreshadowing of the coming of the Messiah and His death on the Cross. So should it be if the greater story of the Incarnation is to be told.

---

[1] As in other critical points in Biblical history, God gives names with specific meanings appropriate to the importance of the occasion.

[2] See my sermon series *The Pain of Christmas*. It may be secured by visiting www.markinc.org or calling 877-markinc.

Harlots & Heroines

The Midwives of the Messiah

- Post a promotional jpg on your web site.
- Give the book to friends, family members or even strangers, as a gift.
- Share a bit about the book and how it touched your life by postings to your web site and blogs
- Write a book review for your local paper, favorite magazine or web site you frequent. Ask your favorite radio show to have the author on as a guest. Media people often give more consideration to the requests of their listeners than the press releases of publicists.
- If you own a business, consider putting a display of these books on your counter where customers will see them. We can make books available for display or resale in quantities as low as 10 at discount rates.
- If you know people (authors, speakers, etc.) who have a voice to the wider culture, ask them if they would review a copy and make a comment on it on their web site or in their newsletters or blogs.
- Talk about the book on email lists you're on, forums you frequent and other places you engage people on the Internet.

Harlots & Heroines

The Midwives of the Messiah

Dr. Chuck Betters

If you've been touched by this book and want to help make it available to others, I invite you to actively participate in its distribution. Word of mouth and personal recommendation are the most effective ways for a book like this to gain attention in both Christian and secular circles. Several suggested methods you can employ are listed on the back of this card.

In the story of Rahab, a professional prostitute and our second Midwife of the Messiah, we will snap a picture for those who believe that God could not possibly love and redeem them due to their great sin. We will see that no man or woman has sunk so low that the Grace of God has not sunk even lower to lift them up.

Chapter 2: Rahab

As we continue our walk through the genealogy of Jesus, leading to that cold, lonely night in a Bethlehem stable, let's meet another unlikely member of that newborn baby's family tree. Her name is Rahab and her contribution in setting the stage for the Incarnation was far from insignificant. Just as baseball players and football players have their "halls of fame," so does the Christian Church have its "hall of fame"—or more accurately, a "Hall of Faith." In the eleventh chapter of Hebrews, the author provides us with that impressive summary of important events in the Old Testament, all of which God brought about through this roll-call of familiar people whose only "claim to fame" was their simple and unforgettable exercise of God-given faith. From among all of the towering figures of Old Testament history, the names and events represented in this Hall of Faith were carefully selected for the purpose of giving us unique insight into the wondrous ways in which God uses broken humanity to accomplish His plan of redemption. Get ready to meet a broken yet miraculously redeemed tool named Rahab.

You will not find any super-heroes or sinless saints among this list of well-known names in the great "Hall of Faith" in Hebrews 11, but rather, ordinary people just like us.[1] They didn't wear a big "S" on their chest; they didn't disappear at will or climb tall buildings like Spider Man. They were real people with real problems, and yet, without downplaying their faults, Hebrews 11 emphasizes some of the more positive snapshots of their lives for our study and consideration. We are referred back to the Old Testament for their life stories as a reminder that they were indeed sinful people who, at critical times, failed miserably. The purpose of Hebrews 11 is not to bring attention or notoriety to the persons themselves or to dwell on their tragedies. It is rather to emphasize the Power, Grace and Mercy of God in spite of human frailties. These stories are about God implementing His sovereign will in bringing to fruition this great truth we know as The Covenant of Grace and of His grafting us, as Gentiles, into His plan to build His Church. As we read Hebrews, we discover a thumbnail history of the Old Testament's critical faith milestones with direct application to our own lives. Practically every personality that should be mentioned in the building of the Covenant story and the miracle of Grace we know as the Incarnation can be found there.

In the middle of this Hebrews 11 Hall of Faith passage, we find the name of another woman who is a revered figure in Israel's history, Rahab. She is prominently mentioned in the genealogy of Jesus in Matthew, chapter 1. As noted in the previous chapter, it was rare that a woman would be included in the male-dominated Jewish genealogies of important people. Nevertheless, God determined, with good reason, that there would be not one, but five women listed in the earthly birth line of Jesus. We can read Rahab's story in the second chapter of Joshua. But first, let's examine Hebrews 11, verse 31: *By faith the prostitute Rahab, because she welcomed the spies, was not killed with those who were disobedient.*

In the context of the New Testament, the letter to the Hebrews was, of course, written to the Jewish people who thoroughly understood the story of Rahab and its implications. They also were intimately familiar with the events of Joshua, chapter 2 that made Rahab a legend in their eyes. This brave woman of Jericho is best known for her decision to hide the spies sent there by Joshua just before God used him to destroy the city. For this reason, her life was spared. Although Hebrews 11 primarily stresses the positive, faithful character of Rahab and other key individuals, their corresponding Old Testament stories pull no punches in laying out the shadier aspects of their lives in excruciating, and sometimes embarrassing, detail.

For example, Hebrews reminds us of the exemplary faith of Abraham in believing and trusting God concerning His Covenant. When we read the Old Testament account of Abraham, however, we see that although he was indeed called by God, his walk with God was seriously hampered by his persistent disobedience. He traveled to Egypt without clear direction from God. He got himself into all manner of trouble there with his lies and deception. In order to save his own skin, he even stooped so low as to offer his wife to another man after claiming she was only his sister. The same hereditary sin pattern of Abraham continued in his son, Isaac, and his grandson, Jacob. Yet, Abraham is one of the "faith heroes" of Hebrews 11, as is Rahab. Go figure, but figure on GRACE!

In an attempt to soften the embarrassment of Rahab's "occupation," some scholars have wrongly chosen to give her the title of "landlady" instead of "prostitute" or "harlot." The term, landlady, is a real stretch in the context of the translation as the Bible makes it abundantly clear that this woman was indeed a prostitute as stated in Hebrews 11:31. Other Jewish scholars attempt to further downplay her dishonorable profession by inferring that she eventually married Joshua, as if this would somehow excuse her earlier behavior. As we read the complete account of Rahab's life we know that she and Joshua never married. She instead married a man named Salmon (Matthew 1:5), son of one of the tribal leaders of Judah. We also know that Rahab, in spite of her questionable reputation, became a respected "Princess of Israel" and a testimony to God's faithfulness.

The account in Hebrews 11 is all about the "Grace focus." Her portrait hangs in the Hall of Faith, blemishes and all, for everyone to see. It is as if God wants to remind us–"This is what she was, and by my Grace, this is what she has become." So again, it is Grace, and not the adulation or condemnation of individual personalities that we are to take away from Hebrews. The author of Hebrews knew exactly how to grab the attention of Jews who were held captive to the belief that strict obedience to the many hundreds of man-made traditions and laws was the only way to gain favor with God. Grace was a foreign concept to them, as it is to any works-based religious system. In studying Rahab's life we have an encouraging and uplifting picture of how God deals with the sins of the past (as well as the present and future) in the lives of His elect.

Make no mistake–God knew every detail of your life when He saved you. In fact, in God's eternal Covenant of Grace, all of your sins–past, present and future–were fully known to Him when He chose to give you new life in Christ. When God in Christ went to that Cross, all of our past was present to Him. When He shed His blood for our sins, there was not one of them in our past, present or future for which He did not specifically die. He loved us with that kind of love. That is Grace! Salvation is all of God and none of man. To believe otherwise is to travel down a dark path to a Godless eternity. Rahab was the recipient of that Grace. The author of Hebrews, a Jew who was very familiar with Jewish audiences, held to the fervent hope that his people would be moved in their hearts to abandon the "highway of works" for the "highway of Grace." Rahab's example, wisely chosen in his letter, would, no doubt, be persuasive.

Rahab's dirty past did not keep her from embracing God's plan for personal forgiveness. The prominent inclusion of Rahab's shameful profession in "The Hall" was not a slip of the pen on the part of the author. The stark contrast between what she was and what she became would have a powerful effect, and offer a ray of hope, for any reader who would wonder how such a sinner could possibly gain favor in the sight of God. Remember, in her immediate circumstances, Rahab had *no* time to "balance" her lifetime of bad works with enough good works; she had not become a master of theology, undergone the rituals of Jewish conversion, or established a long track record of faithful synagogue attendance. What a perfect opening for presenting to the lost, the Christ born in Bethlehem and the reason for which He came.

Having looked at why Rahab appears in the Matthew genealogy and the Hall of Faith the way that she does, let's get to know this intriguing woman a little better through her story in the Old Testament:

Then Joshua son of Nun secretly sent two spies from Shittim. "Go, look over the land," he said, "especially Jericho." So they went and entered the house of a prostitute named Rahab and stayed there. The king of Jericho was told, "Look! Some of the Israelites have come here tonight to spy out the land." So the king of Jericho sent this message to Rahab: "Bring out the men who came to you and entered your house, because they have come to spy out the whole land." But the woman had taken the two men and hidden them. She said, "Yes, the men came to me, but I did not know where they had come from. At dusk, when it was time to close the city gate, the men left. I don't know which way they went. Go after them quickly. You may catch up with them." (But she had taken them up to the roof and hidden them under the stalks of flax she had laid out on the roof.) So the men set out in pursuit of the spies on the road that leads to the fords of the Jordan, and as soon as the pursuers had gone out, the gate was shut. Before the spies lay down for the night, she went up on the roof and said to them, "I know that the Lord has given this land to you and that a great fear of you has fallen on us, so that all who live in this country are melting in fear because of you. We have heard how the Lord dried up the water of the Red Sea for you when you came out of Egypt, and what you did to Sihon and Og, the two kings of the Amorites east of the Jordan, whom you completely destroyed. When we heard of it, our hearts melted and everyone's courage failed because of you, for the Lord your God is God in heaven above and on earth below. Now then, please swear to me by the Lord that you will show kindness to my family, because I have shown kindness to you. Give me a sure sign that you will spare the lives of my father and mother, my brothers and sisters, and all who belong to them, and that you will save us from death." "Our lives for your lives!" the men assured her. "If you don't tell what we are doing, we will treat you kindly and faithfully when the Lord gives us the land." So she let them down by a rope through the window, for the house she lived in was part of the city wall. Now she had said to them, "Go to the hills so the pursuers will not find you. Hide yourselves there three days until they return, and then go on your way." The men said to her, "This oath you made us swear will not be binding on us unless, when we enter the land, you have tied this scarlet cord in the window through which you let us down, and unless you have brought your father and mother, your brothers and all your family into your house. If anyone goes outside your house into the street, his blood will be on his own head; we will not be responsible. As for anyone who is in the house with you, his blood will be on our head if a hand is laid on him. But if you tell what we are doing, we will be released from the oath you made us swear." "Agreed," she replied. "Let it be as you say." So she sent them away and they departed. And she tied the scarlet cord in the window. When they left, they went into the hills and stayed there three days, until the pursuers had searched all along the road and returned without finding them. Then the two men started back. They went down out of the hills, forded the river and came to Joshua son of Nun and told him everything that had happened to them. They said to Joshua, "The Lord has surely given the whole land into our hands; all the people are melting in fear because of us." (Joshua 2:1-24)

Note in this passage the apparent contradictions in Rahab's character. She was a professional woman of ill repute, a pagan and a Canaanite, and yet she displayed an amazingly accurate knowledge of the things that the God of Israel had done for His people. Not having experienced these events first hand, she accepted by faith that they were nonetheless true. Thus, she reverenced their God even though she did not yet know Him. Although many in Jericho also knew of and feared the Hebrew God, the account shows that only Rahab openly confessed a saving faith in Him. The contradiction is amplified by hearing her refer to God in terms of His Covenant name, Yahweh, and yielding to Him as the *God in heaven above and on the earth below.* What an astounding profession of faith for a woman in her position. You see, what saved

Rahab is the same thing that saves us–heartfelt confession of God's Graciousness, God's sovereignty and God's deliverance.

We are saved when, by the power of His Holy Spirit, we come to understand that God, and God alone, provides for our salvation. Jesus is that ram caught in the bush on Mt. Jehovah-Jihreh. It was on this mountain that God promised Abraham, who was about to offer his son Isaac, that He would provide Himself—that is, God Himself would become the sacrifice—for the sins of His people (Genesis 22:1-14).

The deliverance we have is due solely to the miraculous invasion of God, an invasion that manifested in the flesh in a dirty stable in Bethlehem. Who would have thought that God would do something so unexpected and out of the ordinary on that marvelous night we have come to know as the first Christmas. Does not Rahab's story prepare us to expect the unexpected from our God? God often invades our lives when we are at the end of our rope and our backs are against the wall. Was the heavenly invasion in Rahab's life—or ours for that matter—any different from the Divine invasion at the shores of the Red Sea? Moses led the people to the end of their rope where mountains stood to the left and to the right of them, the Red Sea ahead and the Egyptian army behind leaving only one way for them to look–up! With Rahab, as well as with so many precious but troubled lives today, the healing can only come when we forsake our own meager efforts and realize we too have no other direction to look but up. Without God's sovereign invasion, whether it was with Moses, Rahab or us, the armies of Satan would swallow us up and enslave us to the sins of the past.

God in His Mercy and Grace invaded the lives of His chosen people, empowered them, redeemed them and set them free. The exploits of the Jewish people were known far and wide. Rahab recognized that it was not the power of the Israelites themselves, but rather the God Who went before them that made them a force to be feared. She was given the Grace to see her hopeless situation and the need to cast her life into the hands of the one, true, living God.

Rahab is very much like us as evidenced by the fact that right after she placed her faith in the God of Israel, she told an elaborate, premeditated, bold-faced lie. She hid Joshua's men and told the enemy that they had escaped. Scholars have struggled with this aspect of Rahab's story and the implications that bear on our behavior as Christians today. However, we have to keep in mind that Rahab was a brand-new believer surrounded by circumstances and personal baggage that were anything but conducive to her being able to grow in the nurture and the admonition of the Lord. Her pagan background certainly was devoid of any knowledge of God's moral laws. She had none of the advantages that we take so much for granted today as new believers. She did not have a spiritual mentor, a Godly grandmother or a fellow church member who would take her under their wings and open the Scriptures to her. She knew only two things–the faithfulness of a Holy God who redeemed and freed His people and that she was tired of her life the way it was. Although she was putting herself at great personal risk by betraying her own people and aligning herself with God's people, she was determined to protect her new friends in any way she could.

Thus, consistent with her old nature, Rahab told a "little white lie." Yet, God used that lie for good. (Where in Scripture have we heard that before?) She was merely trying to deceive the enemy to protect Joshua's men, which we would view as a normal and acceptable practice in wartime. In addition, she seems to have been counted as righteous for the lie she told (James 2:25). Let us be careful not to judge Rahab for the same behavior for which we have been guilty. Nor should we ever use these Biblical "Grace-encounters" to rationalize our own personal sin (Romans 6:1-2). And though she was without excuse, we must humbly step back and allow Rahab's sin to come under the same Blood that pulled us out of the gutter and washed our own sins away. So, as both a sinner in God's sight and a hero in man's sight, she was given a place in the Savior's family tree.

For perspective here, we should understand that by modern standards, the city of Jericho was very small in both physical size and population. Researchers and archeologists estimate that it was approximately the length of one football field wide by two football fields long, totally enclosed by a sizable wall. People were literally living on top of each other in crowded, multi-level buildings. Everyone in the city knew everyone else. Rahab's house was built into the wall, the same infamous wall God would miraculously bring down via Joshua's army. Since prostitution was considered by many to be a respectable business in Jericho society, it was not unusual to see men coming and going at her house on a regular basis, thus providing a perfect cover for Joshua's spies. She was not looked down upon or considered immoral in any way. She was probably quite wealthy. Her "business activities" would not have drawn the undue attention of the local authorities.

For travelers passing through the region, the well-known city of Jericho was a stop-over point for many travelers. Strangers entering and leaving the city were a very common sight and of little concern to the local citizens. Although we are not given the exact reason how, we are told early on that Joshua's two men were recognized as spies (Joshua 2:2) in spite of their convenient anonymity. In all likelihood, they drew attention to themselves by their obvious curiosity as they roamed the streets showing interest in things that would have been ignored by the average visitor. When agents from Jericho's "FBI office" arrived and knocked on Rahab's front door, her life was destined to be forever changed.

Rahab's home life and her business world were all wrapped into one drama-filled setting—living in a godless city, comfortable and respected in an immoral lifestyle and suddenly invaded by the God of Israel. Through one act of righteousness, and in the exercise of God-given faith, a lifetime of sin was transformed into a timeless example of faith and Godliness. To our modern-day works-oriented thinking, we might unfairly view this as a "foxhole conversion" on her part. However, according to God's definition of sin, our lives are no different from Rahab's when He stepped in and saved us. Were our early Christian years any less plagued than Rahab's by the baggage we brought with us? With a sin-bound life reclaimed by a merciful God, Rahab ended up being favorably compared with the Jewish Old Testament hero, Abraham. Are we not we glad that our God is the God of the second chance! In the New Testament book of James we read:

Was not our ancestor Abraham considered righteous for what he did when he offered his son Isaac on the altar? You see that his faith and his actions were working together, and his faith was made complete by what he did. And the scripture was fulfilled that says, "Abraham believed God, and it was credited to him as righteousness," and he was called God's friend. You see that a person is justified by what he does and not by faith alone. In the same way, was not even Rahab the prostitute considered righteous for what she did when she gave lodging to the spies and sent them off in a different direction? As the body without the spirit is dead, so faith without deeds is dead. (James 2: 21-26)

Both Rahab and Abraham proved to possess a living faith–that is, a faith that produced fruit. They were *not* awarded their faith *because* of their actions or good deeds; rather, their actions were evidence of a faith God had *already* given them. The theological debate of whether one is saved by works or saved by faith is frivolous since it is not an either/or proposition. On the contrary, the two assertions cannot be separated, which is a powerful truth that Rahab's story brings into sharp focus. The Bible, and especially the Letter of James, emphasizes that our faith is dead, or literally non-existent, without evidence in our day-to-day behavior. James stressed the dynamic interrelationship between God-given, saving faith and the resulting works that prove it. In other words, we are not saved *by* our works; we are saved by a faith *that* works (James 2:14-17). Do not be surprised, Christian, if the evidence of your faith may occasionally call for works that are sacrificial and very costly.

In Genesis 22, we read the story of Abraham who, in unhesitating obedience to God, was moments away from killing his son in a repulsive act of human sacrifice. He could have easily claimed intellectual faith all day long, but until he picked up that knife and held it to Isaac's throat, what inspiring evidence would there have been for succeeding generations that Abraham truly trusted and obeyed God regardless of personal cost. For this reason, Abraham is called God's friend.

Rahab enthusiastically recited to Joshua's spies a long list of facts about God and His dealing with the Jewish people and their enemies, even though she had not witnessed the events personally. She did not stop at the level of "intellectual faith," that is, a head full of useless knowledge *about* God. She *believed* God and transferred her trust from position and possessions to the God of the Covenant–"I believe in your God. I've seen what your God has done. I hear the stories of His deliverance. Your God has become my God." Rahab did not merely "talk the talk," she put her life on the line. She knew the city was going down and she and her family with it. She knew there was going to be great calamity and bloodshed, but it did not matter to her. She had already made her choice and aligned herself with the people of God. In so doing, she risked losing the comfort and security of life in Jericho and perhaps her own life. She became a traitor to her own people and fully identified herself with God's people. Her faith was proven to be genuine.

The faith of Rahab and Abraham proved to be genuine. Both were given a place in the genealogy of Jesus as well as special mention in James. Imagine–the harlot, Rahab, is listed right alongside Abraham, the father of the Jewish nation and the greatest of the Old Testament saints. Scandalous? No, Grace!

Do you believe *about* God or do you believe *in* God? There is a big difference. When we believe about God, we become selective and adopt a lifestyle of picking and choosing in matters of obedience. We obey the easy or convenient and we ignore the hard and inconvenient. We say we love God but hate our spouse or exasperate our children. We say we love God but don't serve Him or His Church. Have you made a difference in anyone's life? James refers to this as dead faith. This is not a faith works (James 2:17).

Was Rahab right or wrong in telling the lie? Some respected modern day scholars have taken the position that she did the right thing. Others have maintained that truth is what matters to God and that she was wrong in telling the lie. If Rahab could have had access to the writings of certain Old Testament Jewish Rabbis, she may have been surprised to learn that they actually allowed for her unique situation, or lying under certain circumstances or conditions. They would cite, for example, the story of Jonathan and how he deceived his father Saul in order to protect David. They would cite the fact that Jeremiah lied as he was instructed to by Zedekiah. They would also point to the great prophet, Elisha, who lied when he led the Syrians into Samaria. The Puritans held to a similar theology by insisting that there are times when the greater evil is *not* to lie and that, under certain circumstances, lying could be permitted if telling the truth might cause a greater harm. All would agree, however, that God does not dole out blank checks to lie.

Yet, the struggle is often not as black and white as one might think. There are times when we have to make choices between two competing evils. A mature believer may understand the pros and the cons of the options at hand and have the wisdom to make a Godly decision. Such a maturation process does not take place unless one is ingesting the Scriptures on a regular basis and trusting the indwelling Spirit of God to continuously guide them. We set ourselves up for great danger when we ignore the disciplines of Grace that establish a two-way communication between God and His people. The study of Scripture is God's way of communicating with us. Prayer is how we communicate with God. To ignore these two disciplines is to forfeit the right to wisdom.

On the complex question of the rightness or wrongness of Rahab's lie, the jury is still out. Her decision to lie jeopardized her entire family. In His sovereign way, God used Rahab's lie to protect the spies and fulfill His God's plans for Jericho. Would He have protected the spies if she had told the truth or remained silent? Of course He *could* have; however, God chose to use that lie to accomplish His greater purposes.

Rahab holds a place in the Hall of Faith and in the genealogy of Christ. Rahab the harlot became Rahab the "princess of Israel." Her story is not about her lie, it is about how she, a pagan harlot and sinner, aligned herself with the people of

God and demonstrated a faith that worked even at great personal cost—a faith that produced results. Though the issue of Rahab's deception and God's apparent blessing on it may remain controversial fodder for theological debates, it does not detract from the central purpose for the telling of her story—that the profession of faith and faith *alone* in Christ by the foulest of sinners is sufficient for salvation. *For it is by grace you have been saved, through faith–and this not from yourselves, it is the gift of God–not by works, so that no one can boast* (Ephesians 2:8-9).

In Rahab's defense, she was a brand new believer and her faith was immature at best. Similarly, history records the fact that John Newton, the man who wrote the beloved hymn "Amazing Grace," was a slave trader. After he was converted in 1748, he wrongly continued working in the slave trade even though he sensed it was immoral to do so. Several years later, after his faith had become more fully informed by the Word of God, he abandoned the shameful practice and became active in the early movement in England to abolish slavery. When a heart is infused with the Spirit of God, it can never remain the same, although the transformation seldom happens overnight.

The Word of God is what convinces and convicts. It is prayer and child-like faith, informed by the disciplined study of Scripture that builds spiritual maturity. Here is a principle you can hang your hat on: *If you are not meditating on the Bible and if you are not praying, you are likely not spiritually maturing.* Stagnation and lethargy in your walk with Christ will always lead to weaknesses in your spiritual armor (Ephesians 6:13-17) and subject you to sharp attacks by the Evil One. Rusty armor is useless; having no armor is insane. As the people of Israel wandered in the wilderness they complained about the manna and water God provided on a daily basis. As they tired of the same diet day after day, all they could think about were the melons and other tasty fruit they had enjoyed while enslaved in Egypt. They soon forgot the bricks without straw and the master's whip on their backs. The temptations and preoccupations of day-to-day life around us will quickly fill the void left by an absence of the Word and prayer. Every day we answer the question–How is the Word going to strengthen my faith today? Anyone struggling with a particular sin problem should ask what role the Word of God plays in his or her life. When we read the stories of the Bible we must see the common bonds we have with those who failed or struggled and discover the practical lessons to be learned. If we fail to do so, then spiritual starvation is inevitable.

What do we do if we find ourselves in a spiritual drought and God seems to be silent? We need to do what the prodigal son did (see Luke 15:11-32): poke our heads up out of the muck and the mire and say, "This is not what life was like in my father's house. Why am I here wallowing in a pig pen? I need to get up and return to my father. I need to return to my God." It is simple and yet profound—get into the Word. Read about the wrong choices other people made and what it cost them. Find out about the positive choices people—like Rahab—made and how they were blessed. These stories are in the Bible for that purpose. We have an advantage and unspeakable treasure that Rahab didn't have—the heart and mind of God written down for all to read—a gold mine, breathed by God, useful for teaching, rebuking, correcting and training in righteousness (2 Timothy 3:16). Rahab, with her new heart for God, would have jumped at the opportunity to have a copy of the yet-to-be-completed Holy Scriptures. We have direct access to His throne of Grace. We need no mediator except the Holy Spirit Who intercedes for us.

In the same way, the Spirit helps us in our weakness. We do not know what we ought to pray for, but the Spirit himself intercedes for us with groans that words cannot express. And he who searches our hearts knows the mind of the Spirit, because the Spirit intercedes for the saints in accordance with God's will. (Romans 8:26-27)

There are times when we do not know how to pray. We cannot adequately express our needs before God with words. The beauty of prayer is that, at times like this, the Holy Spirit intercedes for us. He takes our case before the Father on that throne of Grace and says, "Don't listen to him. He doesn't know what he is talking about. He thinks he needs this but he really needs that." There are times when we do all the right things—we pray, study the Scriptures, examine our hearts and confess all known sin to God, but our situation worsens. At times like this we must believe God is at work behind the scenes. The Apostle Paul had this in mind when he wrote, *Put on the full armor of God, so that when the day of evil comes, you may be able to stand your ground, and after you have done everything, to stand* (Ephesians 6:13).

Rahab said to the spies, *I know that the Lord has given this land to you and that a great fear of you has fallen on us, so that all who live in this country are melting in fear because of you* (Joshua 2:9). She then cited examples of specific events in Jewish history. How did she know all of this without having the Scriptures? Most likely, she heard stories from the traveling merchants she encountered in her brothel. She knew of the great miracles of God and the Exodus from Egypt after the 430 years of Israel's bondage. She knew of the well-defined moral code of monotheism, a belief in One God. As one who was raised in the confusion of polytheism (the worship of many gods), belief in this God would have been attractive to her. She perceived that the spies were impeccably moral men of solid character, obviously something to which she was not accustomed. They were not there to pay for one of her girls, but instead, to attend to Divine business. In her country, continuous, wide-spread immoral behavior was the norm. Prostitution was a part of daily life and the corrupt foundation upon which Jericho was built and, up to that point, happily thrived. Rahab's belief system was formed in a crucible of paganism. She grew up in a formidable fortress of immorality, not unlike the world we live in today. To find people like the Jews who worshipped one God and lived by a code of absolute moral standards was indeed both refreshing and appealing to her. As far as she was concerned, Joshua 2:9 tells us, she'd heard enough. It was a done deal. She said she knew the Lord had given them this land. In her new-found faith, she was already seeing things from God's perspective.

All that remained was for a "minor" battle to be fought, but the war had already been won.

Rahab's faith is listed in Hebrews 11 directly by name while Joshua's faith, the guy who obediently marched around Jericho turning the city into a pile of rubble, is mentioned indirectly. Rahab's faith was child-like, simple and uncomplicated. Joshua had the benefit of a direct conversation with God Who promised him victory wherever he went (Joshua 1:1-9). Despite this promise he still had doubts. He had to check out the city for himself. Joshua's decision to send in spies, even after God had told him that the city was already delivered into his hands, was questionable at best. There were no instructions from God for Joshua to send in the spies. God never said, "Go check out the city just to make sure everything I'm telling you is the truth." Perhaps he could have used a little of Rahab's child-like faith. Just a thought!

What does this intriguing and clandestine operation that occurred in a tiny city in ancient Canaan have to do with how we live our lives today?

In the story of Rahab we see clearly that our God is sovereign and we can trust Him. At the top of the list here is something to ponder. What if Joshua had truly believed God about the sure victory over Jericho and had *not* sent spies into the city? In this scenario, Rahab would not have had any spies to hide. Would she still have been rescued and taken to live in Israel to become the mother of Boaz and secure her place in the genealogy of the Messiah? We can only conclude that our sovereign God orchestrated and used an intricate series of human failures and poor decisions to bring His foreordained plan of salvation to fruition. If it had happened any other way, it would have been because He planned it another way—and it is certain the Incarnation still would have happened. God does *not* prepare for "contingencies" and keep a "Plan B" up His sleeve just in case man does not cooperate. If He did, He would not be God. Rejoice friend—God is truly in control and His ways are higher than ours.

Rahab only needed to hear of two of the miraculous acts performed by the Hebrew God—the crossing of the Red Sea and the defeat of the two kings of the Amorites. "God worked miracles among your people. That is good enough for me," she thought. Although she did not witness either of these things directly, she accepted them by faith.

In the story of Rahab we learn that God calls us to live out our lives by simple child-like faith, not by feelings or even by what appears to be reasonable. One can be religious without demonstrating faith. We Christians were not there when Christ was crucified, but we say we believe it. We were not there when He rose from the dead, but we proclaim it to the world. God did not appear to us face-to-face or in a burning bush and say, "I want you saved today." We did not see a blinding light that knocked us to the ground as was done to the Apostle Paul on the road to Damascus. Like Rahab, we simply exercised child-like faith. For the most part we came to faith in Christ because He spoke to our hearts as He used the Word and the piercing conviction of His Holy Spirit to draw us. God gave us the ability to see our hopeless condition against the backdrop of His Holiness. He showed us the hell that was to be shunned and the heaven that was to be gained. We believe Jesus died on that Cross in our place, was buried in that tomb, rose victoriously from the grave and ascended into Heaven. We believe He sent His Holy Spirit in time to reveal God's Word to us. He answered the petitions of those who pleaded to God on our behalf to touch our hearts and bring us to the foot of the Cross. We are the temples of His Holy Spirit and are convinced that He will come back for us, either in death or at His Second Coming. No heavenly figures appeared to us in person and told us about Jesus. We simply placed our faith in what God has done and in what He has promised. That was Rahab's faith. That is our faith. The only difference between Rahab's child-like faith and ours is that she lived before the Cross while we live after the Cross.

Matthew 21:31 says:

"Which of the two did what his father wanted? The first, they answered. Jesus said to them, I tell you the truth, the tax collectors and prostitutes are entering the kingdom of God ahead of you. For John came to show you the way of righteousness and you did not believe him, but the tax collectors

and prostitutes did. And even after you saw this, you did not repent and believe him."

Matthew 23:27-28 says:

"Woe to you, teachers of the law and Pharisees, you hypocrites! You are like whitewashed tombs, which look beautiful on the outside but on the inside are full of dead men's bones and everything unclean. In the same way, on the outside you appear to people as righteous but on the inside you are full of hypocrisy and wickedness.

In this passage, Jesus addressed religious people who had tons of theology crammed into their brains, but not an ounce of Rahab's faith. He in essence told them, "You claim you have all of this knowledge, attend Temple services daily and appear to the unsuspecting to be pious and self-righteous. However, you are just like that sepulcher, that grave in the cemetery. The grave is washed in white and it looks clean on the outside, but if you open it up it is filled with dead men's bones." These teachers and Pharisees knew they had crossed the line. They knew the Law of Moses. No one had to convince them of their sinfulness. What they didn't know was how to gain God's forgiveness.

The difference between what the Pharisees believed and what Jesus actually taught the people was this: The Pharisees said, "Clean yourself up and maybe we will let you into the Inner Court, but not if you're a woman, and you can only go so far if you're a Gentile. If you really want to go all the way and become a good Jew or a God-fearer, then you must be circumcised, follow the rules and regulations and do everything we tell you to do. We set the standards around here—and maybe we will let you move up a couple of pews." Jesus exposed that as hypocrisy and said, "You know, the tax collectors and the prostitutes who have taken a simple step of faith will get into heaven before you, if you get there at all." Rahab did not understand a lot of theology but she understood enough to act upon what she did know. She trusted God and she acted on that trust.

Jesus ran into this kind of prejudice when He encountered the Samaritan woman at the well (John 4:1-43). That encounter went something like this: "What are you doing talking to this woman?" He was asked by His disciples. "What's wrong with you? Don't you know that she is a Samaritan woman and they are nothing but dogs? Furthermore, she has had illicit affairs with almost every man in town—she is an out of control sinner." Jesus asked her for something to drink. When she questioned the propriety of that request, *Jesus answered her, "If you knew the gift of God and who it is that asks you for a drink, you would have asked him and he would have given you living water"* (John 4:10). After an intense dialogue with Jesus, the woman realized that she had been talking to the Messiah. She immediately ran into town and told everyone she could find, "Come and see what I've just seen."

Similarly, God awakened faith in Rahab who risked the consequences by stepping out in that faith. More so than many of those around them, both Rahab and her New Testament sister at the well, understood and lived out an eternal principle—without faith, it is impossible to please God.

The story of Rahab is a testimony to God's self-imposed amnesia. How often do we encounter people who insist that the "dirt" in their past precludes them from any involvement in the church? They often say, "I'm just not good enough to come to church." If they are not merely searching for an excuse, we must commend them for their honesty. This attitude represents a common misunderstanding of what God's Grace is all about and betrays a shallow grasp of what sin really is in God's eyes. If they understood the holiness of God and His hatred of evil, they would have to wonder why we as "church-goers" feel at all worthy to darken the doors of any church. God's truth is that we come to Christ *because* we are unclean. We need forgiveness *because* we are guilty. We need cleansing *because* we are dirty. We need healing *because* we are sick. Satan's MO is to make one feel that he or she must clean up their act first before they come to Christ. If that is where you are in life, ask yourself this question: "How will I know when I am clean enough to approach this Holy God on my terms?" We need to come to Christ because He is the only source of forgiveness. Our past and well-intentioned choices have shaped our present spiritual identity. The sooner we learn that we are completely incapable of healing the chasm we have created between ourselves and this holy God, the sooner we will comprehend and embrace what Jesus meant when He said, *"Come to me, all you who are weary and burdened, and I will give you rest.* (Matthew 11:28). That is a present and eternal rest that the world simply cannot offer.

The story of Rahab teaches us how to face the many critical decisions and forks in the road that will affect and shape our future. If we were to look humbly at the events in the lives of the faith heroes of Hebrews 11, we would be sure to find self-centeredness and poor decision-making, not unlike that of many of us today. Pastors, counselors, church leaders and elders often encounter folks who have seemingly stayed up many nights concocting personal, self-destructing strategies that inevitably lead to serious personal consequences. The counselor will scratch his head and wonder how in the world they got from point A to point B and managed to bring about so much conflict, tension and disarray into what seemed to be the normal lives they were enjoying. If only they could hit the reset button of their lives. Perhaps they would then discern the Biblical principles they violated and identify the habits and sin patterns that must be un-learned. After all of this careful counseling interaction, one must come to a point of recognizing that no progress will be made until the individual takes ownership and admits, *Yes, I made some bad choices. My past has brought me to where I am today. There is nothing I can do about my past. It cannot be changed and it is self-defeating to mourn and wallow in regret and self pity. I can either learn from my poor decisions or live in bondage to my past for the rest of my life. I must begin today to make Godly decisions that will positively affect my tomorrow in a way that will glorify God.*

Isn't it tempting to imagine how different the lives of our Hall of Faith heroes might have been if they had been counseled and coached along the way in Godly decision-making?

Oh, but they *were* counseled and coached. Most of them had the benefit of repeated, close-up and personal, eye-to-eye counseling sessions with the very Lord of Creation that we could only dream about today–and they *still* messed up. Honestly, can we really say we would have done any better? If God chose to use these busted clay vessels to accomplish His perfect will, then He can use you as well!

The story of Rahab teaches us that, just as she stood by her faith decision when she hung out the scarlet thread, so we must also look in faith to Jesus as our scarlet thread and Passover Lamb. *Now she had said to them, "Go to the hills so the pursuers will not find you. Hide yourselves there three days until they return, and then go on your way." The men said to her, "This oath you made us swear will not be binding on us unless, when we enter the land, you have tied this scarlet cord in the window through which you let us down, and unless you have brought your father and mother, your brothers and all your family into your house. If anyone goes outside your house into the street, his blood will be on his own head; we will not be responsible. As for anyone who is in the house with you, his blood will be on our head if a hand is laid on him. But if you tell what we are doing, we will be released from the oath you made us swear."* (Joshua 2:16-20)

And, in the heat of battle, after the walls had collapsed we read:

....The young men who had done the spying went in and brought out Rahab, her father and mother and brothers and all who belonged to her...Then they burned the whole city and everything in it...But Joshua spared Rahab the prostitute...because she hid the men Joshua had sent as spies to Jericho—and she lives among the Israelites to this day. (Joshua 6:23-25)

The story of Rahab is marvelously reminiscent of the story of the first Passover. God had instructed the Jews to smear the blood of a sacrificed lamb on their doorposts so that, when the Angel of Death entered Egypt, their entire household would be passed over." In faith, they hung out that scarlet thread.

The consistent theme of the redeeming Blood of Christ runs literally, as well as symbolically, through every book of the Bible. Tamar's newborn son, Zerah, wore a *scarlet* thread around his wrist (see Genesis 38:27-30) and, as a result, circumstances came together that put Tamar, another one of our Faith Heroes, into the genealogy of Jesus (see chapter one herein). Coincidence? That word is not in God's dictionary.

The scarlet thread and the Passover blood are foreshadows of the Blood of Christ Who is our Passover Lamb and our Scarlet Thread. Hang out the blood for the Angel of Death is coming! When that Angel comes, he is going to be looking at the doorpost of your heart. He is going to be looking for that long scarlet thread. Is your scarlet thread securely in place? Is your Passover prepared? Rahab's faith became legendary in Israel, and rightly so. For the one life-saving faith-decision she made, after a lifetime of separation from God, she became a princess of Israel. Stumbling faith became saving faith. What an infinitely-high premium our God places on that little word, faith.

The story of Rahab teaches us that God honors true faith in His time. In her practical and heart-warming book, *Treasures of Encouragement,* my wife Sharon writes:

> *Rahab had much to learn about this God to whom she had committed her life. How would the women of Israel respond to this tainted woman? It is interesting to see that the Israelites didn't seem to know quite what to do with their Canaanite heroine. "They brought out her entire family and put them in a place outside the camp of Israel" (Joshua 6:23). I can imagine that at least one woman in the Israelite camp, perhaps the mother of one of the two spies, accepted Rahab as a sister. Maybe she insisted that Rahab, who had so bravely welcomed and protected those two men, should not remain "outside the camp" but should become a full member of the covenant community. However it happened, Rahab found her way*

to inside the camp where she found a safe place to learn the ways of Yahweh and His people.[2]

Rahab's act of faith identified her with the people of God; she knew that her only hope lay in journeying with them, since she had literally lost all her possessions and would have to begin life over again. Rahab was given a second chance; she was able to put her past behind her and enjoy a whole new life. She was eventually brought into the family of no less a person than Nahshon, head of the entire clan of Judah (Numbers 1:7, 16; 7:10-17; Matthew 1:4-5). Nahshon was one of the twelve princes who made a special offering at the raising of the tabernacle in Numbers, chapter 7. Rahab married one of his sons, Salmon, and they became the parents of a man named Boaz. Boaz married Ruth and they gave birth to the line of David that continued down to the Incarnation of the Messiah. Imagine that—a prostitute from the land of Canaan becomes a believer and ends up as a critical link in the birth line of the Messiah.

...Ram, the father of Amminadab, Amminadab the father of Nahshon, Nahshon the father of Salmon, Salmon the father of Boaz, whose mother was Rahab, [There she is in the genealogy.] Boaz the father of Obed, whose mother was Ruth, Obed the father of Jesse, and Jesse the father of King David.... (Matthew 1:4-6a; emphasis added).

From there, the genealogy winds its way directly to a young couple huddled beside the manger in Bethlehem—directly into our joyous celebration of that first Christmas Eve. What a marvelous demonstration of the transforming Grace of God. We watch with awe the rise of a woman who overcame, by faith, a sordid and ugly past to become royalty, a forebear of the very King of Kings.

From Rahab the prostitute to Mary the virgin, salvation is not based on how clean you are, but on sheer pure Grace. Her name, Rahab, means "there is room." This inspired the great church father, Origen, to proclaim, "In her name is the message—there is room at the Cross for you."

[1] Betters, Dr. Chuck, *Treasures of Faith: Living Boldly in View of God's Promises* (Phillipsburg, N.J.: Presbyterian and Reformed Publishing Company, 1999).

[2] On the critical importance of the ministry of encouragement see Betters, Sharon W., *Treasures of Encouragement: Women Helping Women in the Church* (Princeton, N.J.: Presbyterian and Reformed Publishers, 1996).

In the story of Ruth, our third Midwife of the Messiah, we will snap a picture of a frightened, grieving widow on a dangerous road to seemingly nowhere. She faced certain poverty and social alienation until the God of Mercy intervened. God used her painful wounds to lay another plank in the miraculous bridge between the promised Seed of the Woman and the fulfillment of that promise, Jesus our Messiah.

Chapter 3, Part 1: Ruth the Moabitess

Ruth. The very mention of her name instantly brings to mind one of the Bible's most poignant and heartwarming stories of love, dedication and loyalty. Her life was definitely not a fairytale story of happiness and privilege. She suffered greatly—and graciously—before God turned her life around. This announcement could very well have appeared in a 1000 B.C. Bethlehem newspaper:

Naomi of the tribe of Judah announces the engagement of her widowed daughter-in-law Ruth, a poverty stricken immigrant from the land of Israel's avowed enemy, Moab, to wealthy Jewish landowner and local businessman Boaz. The prophets from Temple Beth-el reportedly say that the happy couple will become the great-grandparents to King David, the future King of Israel and ancestor to the Messiah. Wedding details to follow.

On a more serious note, this gentle woman was anything but stereotypical material for sensationalism and prurient curiosity. In fact, considering the events of her entire journey, she gives traditionally derogatory mother-in-law stories a new and Godly meaning. Generations have looked back at her life with nothing but the deepest admiration and respect for her as an exemplary woman of faith–a woman who embodies the very definition of the words love, obedience and loyalty.

Have you ever prayed for patience? Have you or someone special in your life ever lost a loved one to that ancient enemy, death? Have you wondered if God could ever lovingly and gently close that chapter of pain and heartbreak and allow you to hear with joy once again the sound of His voice? As we take a short walk with Ruth in the following pages, she might have a word or two for us–if we listen closely. You see, she has been there. She walked in the valley of the shadow of death. She knew loneliness and fear. She knew what it was like to crawl on her face before God and trust Him in spite of her circumstances.

We find this almost-obscure book of Ruth, only eighty-five verses long, right after the book of Judges in the Old Testament. In the final chapter of that era of the Judges, we read of some of the darkest times in Israel's history–their spiritual cycles of great victory followed by great moral failure. At the low point in each failure, God raised up a Judge to lead them back once again into His favor. These cycles inevitably culminated in human disaster on a national scale that is summed up by that ominous verse, *In those days Israel had no king; everyone did as he saw fit* (Judges 21:25). What an indictment of a people who, unlike any other in history, had the advantage of the literal mind and companionship of Almighty God Himself miraculously in their presence.

When we grasp the context and strategic placement of Ruth's story, we will understand clearly that we do indeed serve a sovereign God who does all things well. As we examine the life of this great woman, her amazing family and the circumstances she overcame, we will be able to identify on some level with the brokenness, pain, and fear–not to mention the ultimate joy–that overwhelmed this legendary woman of faith.

There are three important points I want to establish as we begin our story.

First, Ruth is a refreshing and uplifting contrast to one of the darkest eras in Jewish history: the period of the Judges. One should study Ruth along with the

Book of Judges since they are contemporary accounts. This can be seen in the opening words of the book, *In the days when the judges ruled, there was a famine in the land, and a man from Bethlehem in Judah, together with his wife and two sons, went to live for a while in the country of Moab* (Ruth 1:1). This heartwarming book was perfectly placed where it is because of its refreshing change of pace following the calamitous era of the Judges. It is such a wonderfully contrasting story of drama, heartache and intrigue ultimately redeemed by love and healing. Ruth is truly a diamond of virtue against a backdrop of dark moral decline—a brook in the way, so to speak, for anyone journeying along the hot, dusty roads of the Old Testament. As the reader comes away from the depressing accounts of one judge after another serving as God's agents of repentance, it's hard not to wonder, almost in a spirit of discouragement, "Why did they not get it? Why did they not seem to truly understand His plan of redemption? How could they have missed the message?" The times in which Ruth lived were characterized by great moral degeneration and apostasy where men craved more and more evil.

Enter the Book of Ruth, the spiritual biography of one unique woman, where we are relieved to discover that God's words did not fall only on deaf ears after all. To this day, He will still speak powerfully to anyone who reads Ruth's story. There we will encounter God's guiding hand in our lives—a hand that holds us firmly in the grip of His holy character and sovereignty.

Second, Ruth provides a perfect image of the ministry of the coming Messiah. Every book of the Bible points us to the Lord Jesus Christ. There is no Old Testament book that does this more beautifully and more eloquently than the Book of Ruth. It is evident throughout Ruth's story that God fashioned a magnificent tapestry of Grace and Redemption. Ruth could catch but a glimpse of that tapestry as she rejoiced in the wonderful life God had planned for her from the beginning. The story of Ruth is a perfect picture of a loving Savior who comforts and heals the spiritually wounded–in His time.

Third, Ruth is a picture of a loving, close-knit family who stood alone and were obedient to the God they served. Compared to the human train wrecks in the Book of Judges, we are shown here a model of family affection and loyalty that we could only hope would characterize our society today. We would be hard-pressed to find anywhere a more gripping picture of God's model for the kind of love a family is to have for one another. Love, loyalty, respect, patience, accountability, servanthood, obedience—it is all there in Ruth's story and more.

Let us join up with Ruth and begin our walk together:

In the days when the judges ruled, there was a famine in the land, and a man from Bethlehem in Judah, together with his wife and two sons, went to live for a while in the country of Moab. The man's name was Elimelech, his wife's name Naomi, and the names of his two sons were Mahlon and Kilion. They were Ephrathites from Bethlehem, Judah. And they went to Moab and lived there. (Ruth 1: 1-2)

The book opens as a deadly famine was ravaging the land in and around Bethlehem. This is the same sleepy little village where King David would one day tend his sheep as a young boy. Here, twenty-eight generations after David, another small band of shepherds would fall on their faces in terror as the night sky above them broke out in a chorus of angelic praise announcing the Incarnation of the Son of God. Bethlehem is truly the "ground-zero" of God's Covenant plan. So much of Old Testament history and prophesy focused on this little patch of Judean real estate. The village was surprisingly unscathed by the overall degeneracy of the period of the Judges that Israel was experiencing elsewhere. Naomi was uninfected by her surrounding heathen neighbors. God placed an invisible hedge of protection around her to insure her appointment with a Divine, yet-to-be-imagined destiny. Little did the inhabitants, and this particular family, know what was about take place. This is the backdrop of Ruth's incredible story.

Naomi's little family of four had made Bethlehem their home. They were very possibly among the original founders of the town. From all accounts they were good folks with rock-solid values and an unshakable faith in the God of Israel. They were indeed a small glimmer of light against a backdrop of spiritual darkness

One couple, Elimelech and Naomi, seem to have been model parents. It must have been tough to raise children during the seemingly-endless period of moral compromise that characterized the age. This is not unlike the challenges faced by parents today who feel as though they are all alone, swimming desperately upstream while trying to raise their families to know, love and fear God. Are the four walls of your home a secure little "Bethlehem" where there is a shield of protection and safety from the more destructive influences of the outside world? This security is in jeopardy every time your children walk out the door. What will they face? An observant parent cannot help but notice that those walls are porous and much of what we hope to keep at bay has actually crept into our Bethlehem. If we are brutally honest, some of this spiritual contamination comes with the baggage we brought along from our earlier lives—issues that, with God's help, we are still struggling to overcome. Although Elimelech's family did not have to contend with the same modern moral threats we struggle with every day, such as the Internet, television and the many godless expressions of media that blanket our culture, they nonetheless had their own moral wars to fight.[1]

Little did this family know that God was about to invade their relative security in a way that would affect them for generations to come. These "scorch marks," as I refer to them, are the events and circumstances that are filtered through the hands of our sovereign God that radically alter the course of our lives. These "scorch marks" can be pleasant or calamitous. Elimelech, Naomi and their boys were uprooted and forcibly relocated by way of a Divine "scorch mark" in the form of a severe famine. How would this tragic story end? Would Elimelech and his family hold to the belief that their God was sovereign and that He could be trusted, or would they crumble under the load?

This was a “targeted” famine brought about by God that drove this specific family, at this specific time, to the land of Moab where His unique plans for them—both bitter and sweet—would continue to take shape. As the story unfolds, it will become obvious that none of the depicted events occurred by chance, fate or mistake. In fact, as this family’s circumstances are revealed with each new verse, there is a sense of Divine destiny playing out in accordance with a foreordained plan. As one reads the Book of Ruth, curiosity builds. What will happen in the aftermath of this family’s accumulating tragedies?

As strange as it might seem, that particular famine in Bethlehem became one link in the chain of events leading to the coming of the Messiah, the promised *Seed of the Woman*, the One Who would crush the head of Satan (Genesis 3:15). This was a pivotal event in the Messianic timeline. The famine, along with the other seemingly-insurmountable struggles faced by Ruth, would lead human wisdom to conclude that she could not possibly manage a role in the coming of the Messiah. As believers in Christ, we know better, or at least, after our travels through the Book of Ruth, we *should* know better.

God does everything for a reason. The meanings of Hebrew names can almost tell the whole story by themselves. We should not be surprised that the name of this Godly patriarch, Elimelech, means “My God is King.” That certainly gives us insight into the principles by which he raised his family. His wife’s name, Naomi, means “The Pleasant One.” She was a woman of great character who loved her God and her family, and demonstrated that very pleasantness by how she served them. Their two sons were named Mahlon (meaning “sickness”) and Kilion (meaning “failing”), both a foreboding of what was to come. Their tribal name, Ephrata, means “fruitful,” an indication of how the story will end.

This family was likely middle-class, with friends and acquaintances from among both the rich and the poor in the area. In Bethlehem, they would have known practically everyone. Their financial condition was such that they could travel and resettle as they did. In our mind’s eye, it is easy to picture this close-knit little family packing up their belongings as the famine intensified and making their way to Moab to start a new life.

God's sovereign invasion was felt again as there was a sad turn of events: *Now Elimelech, Naomi's husband, died, and she was left with her two sons* (Ruth 1:3). Our hearts must go out to her, but as devastating as this was for Naomi, she still had some security because her sons remained with her and would take care of her. Without them to provide for and protect her, her existence as a widow would have been about as disastrous as it could get. She had lost her husband, her soulmate, the leader of her home, the man who had developed the character of her home and the character of the people of faith who lived there. As Naomi was working through her grief, life in Moab at least seemed to settle into some semblance of normalcy as her sons decided to marry. *They married Moabite women, one named Orpah and the other Ruth* (Ruth 1: 4).

The sons and their wives, no doubt continuing their compassionate care for Naomi, all seem to have done quite well during the ten or more years since they moved to Moab. Life stabilized for them again. The above passage makes a point of stating that the sons both married *Moabite* women. Based on the Godly reputation of Naomi's family and the solid foundation of trust and loyalty they shared together, it is reasonable to assume that Orpah and Ruth embraced, early on, all that their husbands stood for, including their family's faith. Ruth's life testimony surely bears this out.

Although we know Ruth came from a Moabite family, the Scriptures are silent on her parentage. The name Ruth means "Rose," which might give us a little insight into what her father once thought of her. Who exactly *was* her father? According to the Midrash, an ancient set of commentaries on the Hebrew Bible it is conceivable that her father was none other than Eglon, the king of Moab, a notorious yet somewhat obscure character in the Old Testament. Although the Midrash does not carry the same authority as does the Bible, Jewish academic sources of this type have frequently proven to be accurate and deserve consideration. Therefore, it would be useful here to review some of Eglon's own history in order to provide a better appreciation for Ruth's troubled background. She would have been culturally and emotionally affected as a Moabite citizen—even if it turned out that Eglon was not her father

For their persistent rebelliousness, God had delivered Israel over to Moab and their King Eglon. In this particular cycle of judgment, God used this oppression and the ministry of Judge Ehud to draw Israel back to repentance. Heavy taxes were levied against the Jews to the point that they became completely subservient to the people of Moab. Eglon's throne was established in, of all places, the city of Jericho. Recall from the previous chapter the events that took place in and around that infamous city, ending in its miraculous fall at the hands of Joshua—and his spies. The city of Jericho was the enemy stronghold that God had led Israel to defeat at the time of the conquest of the Promised Land. Jericho's strong walls blocked the way into the land of blessing that God had promised to His people. The defeat of Jericho opened up the whole central portion of the Promised Land. However, the industrious and defiant people of Jericho rebuilt the city and, as if in a gesture of revenge for Israel's earlier victory, elevated this man, Eglon, to be their king.

Once again the Israelites did evil in the eyes of the Lord, and because they did this evil the Lord gave Eglon king of Moab power over Israel. Getting the Ammonites and Amalekites to join him, Eglon came and attacked Israel, and they took possession of the City of Palms. The Israelites were subject to Eglon king of Moab for eighteen years. (Judges 3:12-14)

The Lord gave Eglon and the Moabites power and control over Israel as a punishment for their faithlessness and evil. God, in effect, delivered Israel over to her enemies, not unlike the way He delivers and will deliver any nation over to their sins. The city of Jericho arose out of the ash heap to once again become the enemy of God. As this drama unfolded, God raised up a deliverer or Judge in the person of Ehud. God commissioned Ehud to deliver a special package to the pagan king Eglon. It is intriguing to note a small and perhaps overlooked detail from the Biblical account:

Again the Israelites cried out to the Lord, and he gave them a deliverer—Ehud, a left-handed man, the son of Gera the Benjamite. The Israelites sent him with tribute to Eglon king of Moab. (Judges 3:15)

A warrior's armament typically included a hidden dagger, usually strapped to the inside of his left leg. To launch an assault, the soldier would reach into his cloak, draw the dagger from his left leg with his right hand and attack his enemy. Thus, a suspecting enemy would normally and carefully watch his potential assailant's right hand whenever it disappeared into his cloak. The Word of God is wonderfully detailed; Ehud the Judge was a "lefty," thus, his dagger would have been strapped on his right leg. Any movement of his left hand would not have caused any suspicion since Eglon would have been watching his right hand.

After strapping on an eighteen-inch homemade mini-sword under his clothing, Ehud set off for the summer palace in Jericho to take the latest installment of Hebrew tribute to the Moabite king. King Eglon ended up being surprised in more ways than one with the Divine message Ehud presented to him. The dramatic events that took place in Eglon's throne room bear careful examination of the details:

Now Ehud had made a double-edged sword about a foot and a half long, which he strapped to his right thigh under his clothing. He presented the tribute to Eglon king of Moab, who was a very fat man. After Ehud had presented the tribute, he sent on their way the men who had carried it. At the idols near Gilgal he himself turned back and said, "I have a secret message for you, O king." The king said, "Quiet!" And all his attendants left him. Ehud then approached him while he was sitting alone in the upper room of his summer palace and said, "I have a message from God for you." As the king rose from his seat, Ehud reached with his left hand, drew the sword from his right thigh and plunged it into the king's belly. Even the handle sank in after the blade, which came out his back. Ehud did not pull the sword out, and the fat closed in over it. Then Ehud went out to the porch; he shut the doors of the upper room behind him and locked them. After he had gone, the servants came and found the doors of the upper room locked. They said, "He must be relieving himself in the inner room of the house." They waited to the point of embarrassment, but when he did not open the doors of the room, they took a key and unlocked them. There they saw their lord fallen to the floor, dead. While they waited, Ehud got away. He passed by the idols and escaped to Seirah. (Judges 3:16-26)

This slain king may have been Ruth's "daddy," the man who had prophetically named his little girl, "a Rose." How tragic! If the Jewish commentaries are correct, Ruth would have lived through these horrific events as she grew up under Eglon's reign. This would have formed part of her traumatic background as a young, impressionable woman before she married the son of Elimelech. Her cruel and bloody childhood may have prepared Ruth for her future introduction to the one, true, Living God and the most merciful side of His nature.

Returning to Ruth's story, while the famine continued to ravage Bethlehem, death invaded Naomi's home two more times: *After they had lived there about ten years, both Mahlon and Kilion also died, and Naomi was left without her two sons and her husband* (Ruth 1:4-5).

Many are all too familiar with this ugly enemy called Death. To be invaded by this enemy can be a life-shattering event and a personal hell on earth. The soul of a home recovers only slowly to a place even remotely resembling normalcy after the "scorch mark" of death has struck. Could Ruth, in her unbearable pain, ever hope to return to a normal life again? Naomi and her two daughters-in-law were about to journey through a faith-crisis minefield. Naomi lost both her husband *and* her two sons, leaving her and her two daughters-in-law alone and stranded in a society where a woman most often needed the protection of a man to survive. Additionally, all three women were *childless*. At first glance, the Levirate law (see chapter one) appeared to be useless to them since there were no men left in the family, no one to carry on the family name and no one to take over the family business. It was an apparently hopeless situation for these women. Ruth was immersed in incredible grief and turmoil, perhaps including flashbacks of a dysfunctional and greedy father who ended up dead over his insatiable lust for wealth. The wonderful memories of married life soon faded into the dark shadows of heartache and suffering as a penniless widow.

It is no wonder Naomi jumped at the opportunity to return to her beloved Bethlehem, the family home she knew so well:

When she heard in Moab that the Lord had come to the aid of his people by providing food for them [the famine was coming to an end], Naomi and her daughters-in-law prepared to return home from there. With her two daughters-in-law she left the place where she had been living and set out on the road that would take them back to the land of Judah. (Ruth 1:6-7)

Jewish custom expected a daughter-in-law to travel with her widowed mother-in-law in order to see her safely to her home, whatever the distance or inconvenience. Once there, the daughter-in-law had the option to stay or return to her own home. Naomi had to face the harsh reality that she might have to roam the streets and beg for a living. Being a woman of Godly character, however, Naomi refused to play on the sympathies of the two girls. She insisted that they return to their homes in Moab. She was sure they would be much better off in their own culture where people spoke their language. She certainly would not entertain any possibility of these girls begging in the streets:

Then Naomi said to her two daughters-in-law, "Go back, each of you, to your mother's home. May the Lord show kindness to you, as you have shown to your dead and to me.

May the Lord grant that each of you will find rest in the home of another husband." (Ruth 1:8-9)

What grace! What selflessness! What other-oriented love! She treated them as if they were her own daughters:

Then she kissed them and they wept aloud and said to her, "We will go back with you to your people." But Naomi said, "Return home my daughters. Why would you come with me? Am I going to have any more sons, who could become your husbands? Return home, my daughters; I am too old to have another husband. Even if I thought there was still hope for me—even if I had a husband tonight and then gave birth to sons—would you wait until they grew up? Would you remain unmarried for them? No, my daughters. It is more bitter for me than for you, because the Lord's hand has gone out against me!" At this they wept again. Then Orpah kissed her mother-in-law good-bye, but Ruth clung to her. (Ruth 1:9-14)

Such was the heart and spirit of Naomi. She was crushed. As a Godly woman in pain, she admitted her true feelings: *The Lord's hand has gone out against me!* One could hardly blame her. She truly believed God had forsaken her completely. She was so resigned to her abandonment that, when she saw some old friends back in Bethlehem, she told them:

"Don't call me Naomi...Call me Mara [bitter] because the Almighty has made my life very bitter. I went away full, but the Lord has brought me back empty. Why call me Naomi? The Lord has afflicted me; the Almighty has brought misfortune upon me." (Ruth 1:20-21)

For Naomi, life had lost all of its meaning. There was no joy left. From her perspective, her life was over and everything had been taken away. She lost everything she loved. Her cry to be called *Mara* or *bitter* was not that of a godless rebel shaking her fist in God's face. It was an acknowledgement of God's sovereignty. Because of Him, her circumstances had changed. She held no anger against Him. She does not curse

God. I hear in her cry the lament of Job's soul, a broken saint with a worshipful heart: *Though he slay me, yet will I hope in him...* (Job 13:15).

The girls were at a defining crossroad. They had to make a critical decision as to what they were going to do with the rest of their lives—follow Naomi into abject poverty or go back home to Moab and try to put the pieces of their lives back together again. One remained and one left:

...Ruth clung to her. "Look," said Naomi, "your sister-in-law is going back to her people and her gods." But Ruth replied, "Don't urge me to leave you or to turn back from you. Where you go I will go, and where you stay I will stay. Your people will be my people and your God my God. Where you die I will die, and there I will be buried. May the Lord deal with me, be it ever so severely, if anything but death separates you and me." When Naomi realized that Ruth was determined to go with her, she stopped urging her. (Ruth 1:14-18; emphasis mine)

This is a pivotal and critical passage, for it defines God's unchanging template for the conversion of a sin-sick soul. This may very well have been Ruth's defining spiritual moment, her conversion. She took her stand and turned her back on all that she was raised with in a pagan Moabite home. She aligned her life, her future and her eternal destiny with the God of Israel. With these memorable words, another plank in the bridge between the promised *Seed of the Woman* (Genesis 3:15) and the fulfillment of that promise in the coming of Jesus, the Messiah, was nailed permanently into place.

With Ruth's conversion came her commitment to go where Naomi went and to embrace Naomi's God. Traveling to Bethlehem, she would soon stand on the very soil on which the manger would one day stand. She would kneel on the same land where the shepherds knelt hundreds of years later. Thus, the continuity of the Messiah's lineage was assured. The very purpose for Christ condescending to the Incarnation could hardly have been verbalized any more clearly. The fundamental requirement for salvation—*repenting and believ-*

ing—in both the Old and New Testaments could not have been more eloquently stated.

Ruth likely went through a hard decision-making process. She could turn back to Moab and continue to enjoy all of the middle-class comforts and privileges to which she was accustomed. She could stick by her old circle of friends and not have to learn a new culture, a new language, or risk meeting new people. She could return to Moab where life would be familiar, stable and predictable, *or* she could turn toward Bethlehem and dare take a leap of faith—a *giant* leap of faith—in the company of this poor, ready-to-beg, bitter, heartbroken, grieving mother-in-law of hers who was not even sure that her God would ever speak to her again. Ruth had nothing on which to base her Bethlehem decision except the character and the role model of Naomi—and a sold-out faith in Naomi's God. There was not even an encouraging promise from God that everything would work out. All that faced these two women was a life of shame and poverty. The decision was made—*Ruth clung to Naomi and Naomi's God.* Orpah returned to Moab, only to disappear from the pages of Scripture.

We can celebrate the true meaning of the Incarnation as we ponder on a few important thoughts gleaned from our time together with our sister, Ruth:

The story of Ruth teaches us that nothing happens to us, no matter how good or how bad, that is not first filtered through the hand of a sovereign God. Even the evil acts of men are subject to the sovereign will of God. Ask Job. Both Job and Ruth would assure us that: *No temptation has seized you except what is common to man. And God is faithful; he will not let you be tempted beyond what you can bear. But when you are tempted, he will also provide a way out so you can stand up under it* (I Corinthians 10:13).

We will need to walk *through* the pain. He did not promise to take it away. Again, ask Job or Ruth. On the contrary, He assured us that we who name the name of Jesus in a fallen world can expect to be attacked. We can watch with certainty for the incoming barbs of our ancient enemy. We are surely promised our Father's ultimate protection while we walk through it. The hardest part of this promise, however, is that God may or may *not* reduce the intensity of the trial. There may only be rare occasions, unbeknownst to us, when He shields us from being hit altogether. It is always His call. Either way, we cannot lose—here *or* in eternity since we cannot out give God. We will often need to reassure ourselves with Paul's comforting words to the persecuted Christians living in Rome:

*Who shall separate us from the love of Christ? Shall trouble or hardship or persecution or **famine** or nakedness or danger or sword? No, in all these things we are more than conquerors through him who loved us. For I am convinced that neither death nor life, neither angels nor demons, neither the present nor the future, nor any powers, neither height nor depth, nor anything else in all creation, will be able to separate us from the love of God that is in Christ Jesus our Lord.* (Romans 8:35-39; emphasis mine)

Are you facing a "faith-size" decision that will prove whether or not you believe in the sovereignty of our God, and that you can trust Him? We face that challenge every day of our lives in matters both big and small. The trustworthiness and sovereignty of our God is one of the foundational messages in all of Scripture. There will be times when we faint under trial or temptation. It is in the aftermath of those failures that we may be tempted to believe that our sins are so great that they are bigger than God's love, bigger than His Grace and bigger than His forgiveness. During those moments, remember this—none of us have sunk so low that our God has not stooped lower to pick us up. This is the truth of the Gospel!

The story of Ruth teaches us that, until we have walked in another person's sorrow, we are unqualified to judge their motives in questioning God's love. When I read the story of Naomi, I don't have a single word of condemnation for this woman. Until one walks in her shoes, one cannot understand the depth of her bitterness and pain.

Stay tuned, for little did Naomi or Ruth know that just around the corner God placed a man named Boaz.

---

[1] For the myriad of challenges facing children today and practical help on how to face them as parents, refer to my book. Betters, Dr. Chuck, *Teaching Them Young: The Hidden Treasures of the Proverbs* (Newark, DE: New Heaven Publishing, 2009).

In the marriage between Boaz, the kinsman-redeemer, and Ruth, the redeemed one, we see a snapshot of an eternal wedding planned in Heaven before the foundation of the world. This elegant marriage is celebrated every time Jesus, our true Kinsman-Redeemer, saves a lost soul and builds His Church, His Bride.

Chapter 3, Part 2: Ruth and the Kinsman-Redeemer

The drama is not over—far from it. There is so much more of God's amazing sovereign control over His eternal plan of redemption to come. Naomi and Ruth had resigned themselves to their fate in the streets of Bethlehem, but a uniquely Jewish social protocol would become the vehicle by which their lives were turned upside down.

As we discussed in the life of Tamar, the law of the Levirate obliged a brother to marry the widow of his childless deceased brother, with the firstborn child being treated as that of the deceased brother, including property ownership and inheritance rights. In Ruth's case, her husband and his brother were dead. There were no other brothers left to assume the responsibility of the law for her protection. That fact brought into play another possible solution to the plight of the widow.

"'If an alien or a temporary resident among you becomes rich and one of your countrymen becomes poor and sells himself to the alien living among you or to a member of the alien's clan, he retains the right of redemption after he has sold himself. One of his relatives may redeem him: An uncle or a cousin or any blood relative in his clan may redeem him. Or if he prospers, he may redeem himself. (Leviticus 25:47-49)

This was the Law of the *Kinsman-Redeemer*. There were four strictly enforced requirements for a man to fulfill this role:

- He must be a kinsman, that is, he must be related to the person he is planning to redeem.
- He must be free himself. A slave was not permitted to redeem another slave. A Kinsman-Redeemer had to be free of debt and bondage.
- He must be able to pay the price to redeem his relative.
- He must be willing to pay the price.

There were a number of slaves with rich uncles who just didn't want to spend the money to release their relatives from slavery. Aside from distant relatives through her deceased husband, Elimelech, Naomi had no immediate next-of-kin to satisfy the obligation of the Levirate and secure her property and family name. But things were about to start looking up:

"So Naomi returned from Moab accompanied by Ruth the Moabitess, her daughter-in-law, arriving in Bethlehem as the barley harvest was beginning. Now Naomi had a relative on her husband's side, from the clan of Elimelech, a man of standing, whose name was Boaz." (Ruth 1:22–2:1)

According to the ancient rabbis, Boaz had just buried his first wife when Naomi and Ruth arrived in town. Whether or not this is true, we cannot say for sure, but the timing does direct our attention to a bigger picture going on behind the scenes. The original Hebrew text for the word *relative* is more literally *an acquaintance*. Boaz was related, albeit not as an immediate next-of-kin. He was a distant relative.

Continuing:

And Ruth the Moabitess said to Naomi, "Let me go to the fields and pick up the leftover grain behind anyone in whose eyes I find favor." ...<u>As it turned out</u>, she found herself working in a field belonging to Boaz, who was from the clan of Elimelech. Just then Boaz arrived from Bethlehem and *greeted the harvesters, "The Lord be with you!" "The Lord bless you!" they called back. Boaz asked the foreman of the harvesters, "Whose young woman is that?" The foreman replied, "She is the Moabitess who came back from Moab with Naomi."* (Ruth 2:2-6; emphasis mine)

More than likely, there were many women in Bethlehem doing the same thing Ruth was doing—begging. Yet, Boaz's eyes fell directly on Ruth. Both the foreman and Boaz knew Naomi, her plight and the undesirable origin of Ruth the Moabitess. The continuous reference to Ruth as a "Moabitess" was not a compliment or a term of endearment. It was a way of branding her with prejudice and contempt for her status as a foreigner. This served only to elevate by contrast the compassionate character evident in Boaz.

"She said, 'Please let me glean and gather among the sheaves behind the harvesters.' She went into the field and has worked steadily from morning till now, except for a short rest in the shelter." So Boaz said to Ruth, "My daughter, listen to me. Don't go and glean in another field and don't go away from here. Stay here with my servant girls. Watch the field where the men are harvesting, and follow along after the girls. I have told the men not to touch you. And whenever you are thirsty, go and get a drink from the water jars the men have filled." At this, she bowed down with her face to the ground. She exclaimed, "Why have I found such favor in your eyes that you notice me—a foreigner?" (Ruth 2:7-10)

Ruth was not as alone in the world as she had imagined. She was on the receiving end of Divine protection. Our God had already gone before her to prepare the necessary balm to bind up her wounds. Unaware of what God was planning behind the scene, she simply acted out of her own Godly character, refused to throw a pity-party and got to work. Ruth's desire was to glorify God *no matter what,* even if there was a huge hole in her heart from the pain of her loss. She kept moving. [God hits moving targets who are fueled by faith.]

Boaz took immediate interest in seeing to it that Ruth was protected and that her needs were met.

In Ruth's question to Boaz—*Why have I found such favor in your eyes that you notice me–a foreigner?* (Ruth 2:10), we are given the template for how we must approach a holy God and bow humbly before Him. As we come to faith in Christ, we should all ask, *How is it, Lord, that I have found favor in your eyes? Why have you even bothered to take a moment's notice of me, a foreigner–an alien to all things holy and righteous?*

Boaz replied, "I've been told all about what you have done for your mother-in-law since the death of your husband–how you left your father and mother and your homeland and came to live with a people you did not know before. May the Lord repay you for what you have done. May you be richly rewarded by the Lord, <u>the God of Israel</u>, under whose wings you have come to take refuge." (Ruth 2:11-12; emphasis added)

The key phrase here is *The God of Israel*–the God with Whom she had aligned herself. Although her faith journey was not over, she was at home in the arms of the God she trusted with her life.

"May I continue to find favor in your eyes, my lord," she said. "You have given me comfort and have spoken kindly to your servant–though I do not have the standing of your servant girls." (Ruth 2:13)

This is not false humility on Ruth's part. She was fully aware of her low estate even in comparison with the servant girls. She had no rights and was totally at the mercy of Boaz and the harvesters.

All the key characters are in place and the stage is set for this unfolding drama. We have arguably watched a greater number of events miraculously come together in one place, at one time, and in the lives of any one group of people, than anywhere else in the Bible. All of these roads converged at this unique place in Old Testament history, and a bridge had to be built, through the life of Ruth, to allow the journey to proceed to the manger. Who could have been a better fit for the spotlight of Biblical history to shine on than this humble woman? It all began in Bethlehem and it would end in Bethlehem!

At mealtime Boaz said to her, "Come over here. Have some bread and dip it in the wine vinegar." When she sat down with the harvesters, he offered her some roasted grain. She ate all she wanted and had some left over. As she got up to glean, Boaz gave orders to his men, "Even if she gathers from among the sheaves, don't embarrass her. Rather, pull out some stalks for her from the bundles and leave them for her to pick up, and don't rebuke her." (Ruth 2:14-16)

This was an amazing gesture of grace and generosity Boaz extended to this Moabitess foreigner who had migrated to his homeland. All food sources were precious at that time, especially considering the devastation caused by the very recent famine. Many hungry gleaners would have been expected to converge on the fields. Jewish custom was to freely allow the beggars, foreigners and outcasts of society to rush in and gather all that they could of the leftovers in order to survive. Once again, Boaz singled out Ruth:

So Ruth gleaned in the field until evening. Then she threshed the barley she had gathered, and it amounted to about an ephah [about 25 pounds]. She carried it back to town, and her mother-in-law saw how much she had gathered. Ruth also brought out and gave her what she had left over after she had eaten enough. (Ruth 2:17-18)

Talk about hard work and industriousness—she labored from early morning until night, picking up scraps, and managed to bring home 25 pounds of barley, corn and other grains. She was allowed to continue this routine day after day. This was beyond her and Naomi's wildest dreams. It is amazing how gently God dealt with Naomi's crisis of faith. She had only recently *felt* certain that her God had abandoned her, taken away all that she had, removed His protection and left her with nothing but bitterness. Then, there stood Boaz who provided protection and abundance for both women. This gracious and generous encounter with Boaz was the pivotal point and the spiritual about-face in Naomi's and Ruth's faith journey.

Naomi once owned land in Bethlehem through her husband Elimelech and lost it in the economic collapse. Land was a vital possession in the Jewish culture and economy. It was so vital that there were laws outlining a process by which land lost to foreclosure could be returned to its original owner. Naomi had the right to expect someone of means to step up to the plate and say to the new owner, "I will redeem this land you now own and return it to this poor widow." This compassionate law demanded that the new owner had to sell the land back to the one who lost it, provided there was a kinsman-redeemer willing to pay for it. Land was expected to remain a family possession forever.

The only other way one could reclaim their land was to wait for Israel's next celebration of the Year of Jubilee that was held every fifty years. During this festival, all debts were retired no matter what was owed. All was forgiven. No matter what you lost, it was returned. Jubilee, however, was too far off to be of any immediate benefit to Ruth and Naomi. Since Ruth had no brother or next-of-kin, the next best thing she had going for her was a distant relative or acquaintance who, it so happened, was a member of her father-in-law's clan. That man was Boaz.

Her mother-in-law asked her, "Where did you glean today? Where did you work? Blessed be the man who took notice of you!" Then Ruth told her mother-in-law about the one at whose place she had been working. "The name of the man I worked with today is Boaz," she said. "The Lord bless him!" Naomi said to her daughter-in-law. "He has not stopped showing his kindness to the living and the dead." She added, "That man is our close relative; he is one of our kinsman-redeemers." (Ruth 2:19-20)

Boaz may have been a distant relative, but from the perspective of these women he was their *brother*, a true kinsman-redeemer. Boaz had no legal obligation to intervene and redeem Naomi's property. He had no moral obligation to do more than protect Ruth in the fields and allow her to gather some food. How would this scene end?

Then Ruth the Moabitess said, "He even said to me, 'Stay with my workers until they finish harvesting all my grain.'" Naomi said to Ruth her daughter-in-law, "It will be good for you, my daughter, to go with his girls, because in someone else's field you might be harmed." So Ruth stayed close to the servant girls of Boaz to glean until the barley and wheat harvests were finished. And she lived with her mother-in-law. (Ruth 2:21-23)

Naomi and Ruth were going to take advantage of the spirit of the law (Deuteronomy 24:19-22) protecting the widow and the alien. Naomi's plan was to allow the relationship between Ruth and Boaz to develop without forcing it and wait on God's timing. After a while, it was time for Ruth to make her next move.

One day Naomi her mother-in-law said to her, "My daughter, should I not try to find a home for you, where you will be provided for? Is not Boaz, with whose servant girls you have been, a kinsman of ours? Tonight he will be winnowing barley on the threshing floor. Wash and perfume yourself, and put on your best clothes. Then go down to the threshing floor, but don't let him know you are there until he has finished eating and drinking. When he lies down, note the place where he is lying. Then go and uncover his feet and lie down. He will tell you what to do." "I will do whatever you say," Ruth answered. So she went down to the threshing floor and did everything her mother-in-law told her to do. (Ruth 3:1-6)

Ruth was about to claim Boaz as her kinsman-redeemer. As he was celebrating the completion of the harvest with his workers, Naomi seized the moment to execute her plan and present the kinsman offer to Boaz. She correctly took his kindness and affection toward Ruth as a signal of his willingness to become the kinsman-redeemer. Naomi was perfectly within her rights to proactively secure a kinsman-redeemer for her daughter-in-law. Because Naomi and Elimelech were forced to sell their Bethlehem property when they fled the famine, the two women had become penniless widows. The conditions were certainly right for a kinsman-redeemer to step up, buy back the property and marry Ruth.

In our modern culture, we might be tempted to accuse Ruth of being on the prowl for a "sugar daddy." We might even accuse Naomi of prostituting her own daughter-in-law. Nothing could be further from the truth given the twin laws of the Levirate and the kinsman-redeemer. Naomi instructed Ruth to follow the custom of laying herself at the feet of the one she thought was to be her kinsman-redeemer. If she had the wrong man, all he had to do was stand up and say so. Guided by the hand of God, Naomi and Ruth were not mistaken about Boaz:

When Boaz had finished eating and drinking and was in good spirits, he went over to lie down at the far end of the grain pile. Ruth approached quietly, uncovered his feet and lay down. In the middle of the night something startled the man, and he turned and discovered a woman lying at his feet. "Who are you?" he asked. "I am your servant Ruth," she said. "Spread the corner of your garment over me, since you are a kinsman-redeemer." (Ruth 3:7-9)

In Ruth's eyes, this could go either way. This was her rightful proposal for Boaz to become her kinsman-redeemer.

"The Lord bless you, my daughter," he replied. "This kindness is greater than that which you showed earlier: You have not run after the younger men, whether rich or poor. And now, my daughter, don't be afraid. I will do for you all you ask. All my fellow townsmen know that you are a woman of noble character." (Ruth 3:10-11)

Ruth could have returned to Moab and found other more culturally conducive prospects there, even a younger man. It was her submissive spirit and love for Naomi that drove her to the feet of Boaz, who lovingly accepted her. There was one problem however.

"Although it is true that I am near of kin, there is a kinsman-redeemer nearer than I. Stay here for the night, and in the morning if he wants to redeem, good; let him redeem. But if he is not willing, as surely as the Lord lives I will do it. Lie here until morning." (Ruth 3:12-13)

Legally, there was another distant relative who held the "right of first refusal." This unnamed man must be given the first opportunity to serve as Ruth's kinsman-redeemer. Then, while carefully shielding her from prying eyes, he gave her some food and sent her away:

So she lay at his feet until morning, but got up before anyone could be recognized; and he said, "Don't let it be known that a woman came to the threshing floor." He also said, "Bring me the shawl you are wearing and hold it out." When she did so, he poured into it six measures of barley and put it on her. Then he went back to town. When Ruth came to her mother-in-law, Naomi asked, "How did it go, my daughter?" Then she told her everything Boaz had done for her and added, "He gave me these six measures of barley, saying, 'Don't go back to your mother-in-law empty-handed.'" Then Naomi said, "Wait, my daughter, until you find out what happens. For the man will not rest until the matter is settled today." (Ruth 3:14-18)

Boaz found the man and the intriguing court proceedings began:

Meanwhile Boaz went up to the town gate and sat there. When the kinsman-redeemer he had mentioned came along, Boaz said, "Come over here, my friend, and sit down." So he went over and sat down. Boaz took ten of the elders of the town and said, "Sit here," and they did so. Then he said to the kinsman-redeemer, "Naomi, who has come back from Moab, is selling the piece of land that belonged to our brother Elimelech. I thought I should bring the matter to your attention and suggest that you buy it in the presence of these seated here and in the presence of the elders of my people. If you will redeem it, do so. But if you will not, tell me, so I will know. For no one has the right to do it except you, and I am next in line." "I will redeem it," he said. Then Boaz said, "On the day you buy the land from Naomi and from Ruth the Moabitess, you acquire the dead man's widow, in order to maintain the name of the dead with his property." At this, the kinsman-redeemer said, "Then I cannot redeem it because I might endanger my own estate. You redeem it yourself. I cannot do it." (Now in earlier times in Israel, for the redemption and transfer of property to become final, one party took off his sandal and gave it to the other. This was the method of legalizing transactions in Israel.) So the kinsman-redeemer said to Boaz, "Buy it yourself." And he removed his sandal. (Ruth 4:1-8)

At first, the unnamed man thought he was getting a real deal—cheap land from a penniless widow—before Boaz reminded him that marriage to Ruth came with the land. The man then realized the financial hit he would take and backed out of the deal. In a characteristic display of responsibility and accountability, Boaz went before the town elders and all the people, announced his plans and enlisted them as witnesses:

Then Boaz announced to the elders and all the people, "Today you are witnesses that I have bought from Naomi all the property of Elimelech, Kilion and Mahlon. I have also acquired Ruth the Moabitess, Mahlon's widow, as my wife, in order to maintain the name of the dead with his property, so that his name will not disappear from among his family or from the town records. Today you are my witnesses!" (Ruth 4:9-10)

The purpose of the Book of Ruth is revealed in one particular phrase in the above passage–*...in order to maintain the name...so that his* [Elimelech's] *name will not disappear from among his family...* Ruth's story is all about preserving the *name.* The legacy could not die because the sons died. It could not die because Elimelech died.

The elders recognized the honorable thing that Boaz had done and gave him the highest possible blessing they could give on his marriage to Ruth along with the prayer that God would give them children to preserve the *name.*

Then the elders and all those at the gate said, "We are witnesses. May the Lord make the woman who is coming into your home like Rachel and Leah, who together built up the house of Israel. May you have standing in Ephrathah and be famous in Bethlehem. Through the offspring the Lord gives you by this young woman, may your family be like that of Perez, whom Tamar bore to Judah." (Ruth 4:11-12)

Can there be any scene more touching than what follows:

So Boaz took Ruth and she became his wife. Then he went to her, and the Lord enabled her to conceive, and she gave birth to a son. The women said to Naomi: "Praise be to the Lord, who this day has not left you without a kinsman-redeemer. May he become famous throughout Israel! He will renew your life and sustain you in your old age. For your daughter-in-law, who loves you and is better to you than seven sons, has given him birth." Then Naomi took the child, laid him in her lap and cared for him. The women living there said, "Naomi has a son." And they named him Obed. He was the father of Jesse, the father of David. (Ruth 4:13-17)

This is what this beautiful story is about—establishing the Davidic line. The Messiah *must* come from the line of David. He *must* become our King just as David became Israel's king. Because of this Divinely-arranged marriage, Jesus Christ held that critical Messianic credential—He was the Son of David.

However, there is more to this story. The great bridge between the *Seed of the Woman* (Genesis 3:15) and the Messiah, the Lord Jesus Christ, included a unique plank of prophecy unrealized before this time. When God formalized His covenant with Abraham, He said:

The Lord had said to Abram, "Leave your country, your people and your father's household and go to the land I will show you." I will make you into a great nation and I will bless you; I will make your name great, and you will be a blessing. I will bless those who bless you, and whoever curses you I will curse; <u>and all peoples on earth will be blessed through you.</u>" (Genesis 12:1-6; emphasis mine)

Did you catch the promise in the last phrase? Not only would the offer of salvation be extended to one nation, Israel, just as God promised Abraham, but the Gospel would also extend beyond the borders of Israel as God built a highway to the Gentiles. The Messiah to come would bring salvation to *all the peoples of the earth,* Jew and Gentile alike. In the eventual marriage of Ruth, a Gentile Moabitess, and Boaz a Jew, the bridge to the Messiah and the highway to the Gentiles came under construction. God's offer of salvation would be extended to the whole world without distinction. Ruth *the Moabitess* is a snapshot of the Church. Boaz the *kinsman-redeemer* is a snapshot of Christ, our eternal Kinsman-Redeemer.

The inklings of this marriage were seen early on when the Jewish sons of Elimelech married Gentiles—two Moabite women. Amazingly, no objections were raised since God had an eternal, inviolate plan in mind. He ordained Boaz and Ruth to be an important link in the genealogy of the Messiah as He Divinely crafted the highway of Redemption to a lost world. We have to simply stand in awe at the breath-taking, Divine orchestration of all that transpired in this landmark book with not an ounce of coincidence in any of it. As one reads this monumental little book, the practical lessons fly off its pages.

The story of Ruth teaches us that God honors character developed in obscurity and through great pain. We could hardly find more exemplary human role models of Godly character in the entire Bible than in Naomi, Ruth and Boaz. Consider Naomi's selfless love in always putting the welfare of her two hurting daughters-in-law ahead of her own. Marvel at Ruth's humility, obedience and her servant's heart toward Naomi and Boaz, as well as her faithful attention to responsibility in spite of her dire circumstances. Gaze at Boaz's generosity and compassion toward a poverty-stricken outcast. He had wealth and power, yet never lost sight of mercy and grace toward the ones who had neither. They all lived out their lives in full view of a holy and loving God.

Ruth was grafted into the family of Boaz just as all of God's children are grafted into God's Covenant family through Jesus. He has made us His Bride. All the rights and privileges that came with that union are ours—the Church's—to enjoy. We in Christ are not spiritual widows and orphans any longer. We live on that highway to the Gentiles that was built through Ruth's story. Through faith in Christ, we enjoy all the privileges that come with being the princes and princesses of the King of Kings and Lord of Lords. We are left to fall to our faces and cry out, *Why have I found such favor in your eyes that you notice me—a foreigner? Why were you even looking for me?* Our God has known us from before the foundation of the world, and He calls His people in His time to know Him. Although we did not seek Him, He sought us, and redeemed us out of the pit. Hallelujah!

The story of Ruth teaches us that the Incarnation is the eternal unveiling of the only One Who is qualified to be our Kinsman-Redeemer. That baby in the manger would, in due time, grow up for the sole purpose of going to a cross to bear your sins and mine. He *redeemed* as only our Kinsman-Redeemer could. As noted toward the beginning of this chapter, in order to qualify as a kinsman-redeemer there were four non-negotiable requirements. Jesus the Christ more than satisfies every one of them:

He must be a <u>kinsman</u>.

That is, he must be related to the one whom he is going to buy back. In this sense, Jesus is our Kinsman-Redeemer. He is our brother.

A kinsman-redeemer must be free of the debt and bondage that fell on the one who was to be redeemed.

Jesus is our Kinsman-Redeemer since He was not enslaved to sin as we are.

A *kinsman-redeemer must be able to pay the price to redeem his relative.*

Jesus is our Kinsman-Redeemer since He alone, as the sinless God-Man, was able to pay the price for our sins.

The kinsman-redeemer must be willing to pay the price.

Jesus is our Kinsman-Redeemer since He willingly laid down His life for His Bride.

When you feel that all is lost, hope is gone and even God has abandoned you, look to the Kinsman-Redeemer. He is the one who has set you free. When you come to the point of saying, *Don't call me Pleasant, call me Mara, call me bitter,* cling to the Kinsman-Redeemer who has promised that He will never leave you, He will never forsake you, and He will never abandon you—even when the lights go out. He is the Kinsman-Redeemer Who set us free and bought back all that Satan stole from us.

The story of Ruth teaches us that God is most present when we do not sense His presence. Three women lost their husbands and lived for years in poverty, begging in the streets. They were forced to adopt the customs and language of a strange land. You can imagine the fear they must have experienced. But our God, behind the scenes, protected them and gently directed them along a path He had prepared for them in eternity past. Surely, in their fear and loneliness these women must have wondered at times of the whereabouts of their God.

The story of Ruth teaches us that every book in the Bible is a Messianic book, from Genesis to Revelation. Even as you read a book such as Leviticus with all of its emphasis on sacrifices, remember that those sacrifices all point to Christ. The Exodus and the Passover point to Christ. The book of Ruth points to Christ. This is as much a story about Jesus as are the books of Matthew, Mark, Luke and John. And this woman is your foremother, your legacy, your roots. As believers, her story is our story.

Our Kinsman-Redeemer has purchased your inheritance with His blood. He is preparing a place for you and has been touching it up for over two thousand years. When all is ready, as He did with Ruth, Boaz, and Naomi God will take you home. There will be no more questions, darkness, pain, sorrow or brokenness. God will not merely remove the sting of death—death itself will be no more. That is the unspeakable hope and joy of the Incarnation and the promise that became reality through the legacy of Naomi, Ruth and Boaz.

In the story of our fourth Midwife of the Messiah, Bathsheba, a beautiful woman married to a brave and loyal soldier, we will snap a picture of hope for those who are the victims of another's bad choices and of how a sovereign God uses our dire circumstances as a platform to declare his Glory.

Chapter 4: Bathsheba

Adam and Eve, Abraham and Sarah, Samson and Delilah, Ruth and Boaz, Joseph and Mary; all of them are practically household names when mentioned together as historically-inseparable couples in the Bible. You can hardly think of any one of these names without also recalling their legendary corresponding "partner." Some of them are famous for all the right reasons. Some should more accurately be described as infamous, that is, deserving of a very bad reputation. Who among these couples deserves such harsh condemnation? What about Bathsheba and her run-in with the most famous king in the Old Testament—King David? As tempting as it may be to accept the popular criticisms of this particular pair, let me encourage you to suspend judgment until after our visit with the "bathing beauty and the royal voyeur" in the following pages.

Christians and historians alike have mixed reactions when the names of David and Bathsheba come up in conversation. Consider the glaring contradictions. David is an enigma—a victorious warrior and a distracted commander, the slayer of Goliath and a fallen adulterer, the protector of the scared Ark of the Covenant and a violator of the very Law it contained, the conqueror of the Promised Land and a broken and defeated sinner. For Bathsheba's part, a previously obscure military housewife was suddenly caught up in a whirlwind of celebrity, scandal and sensationalism. How could a Holy God possibly refer to David as *a man after His own heart* (1 Samuel 13:14)? For that matter, how could He assign this tarnished couple a prominent part in the Messiah's family tree?

Since God sees His children through the eyes of His Son, Jesus Christ, we are always the objects of His great love even though we might morally fail. He sees the entirety of one's life and not merely his or her failures, from our sin-soaked beginnings to our ultimate rest in heaven. How could a Holy God look at you and me, call us sons and daughters, and love us with an everlasting love? God wrote our life stories in eternity past. Every step you have taken, from your birth to your home-going, has been filtered through His sovereign hand. *In his heart a man plans his course, but the Lord determines his steps* (Proverbs 16:9). So it was with David and Bathsheba.

The story details Bathsheba's encounter with her king whom she had always trusted and admired. The drama showcases the exploits of a man and a woman whose lives were radically altered in minutes by one of the most notoriously-bad decisions recorded in the Scriptures. At the same time, it is also a vivid portrait of God's redeeming love.

Bathsheba was the unpretentious wife of a skilled, professional soldier. Her husband, Uriah, held a position in the military chain of command that likely warranted a privileged housing location "Inside the Beltway." He and his wife found themselves living practically next door to a real celebrity, the Commander-in-Chief, the legendary King David himself. This physical proximity would prove to be more of a curse than a blessing.

Was Bathsheba a temptress, an innocent victim, or something else? There are two fundamental Biblical realities that underlie the story of Bathsheba.

One—*The heart is deceitful above all things and beyond cure. Who can understand it* (Jeremiah 17:9)?

The other—*I know that nothing good lives in me, that is, in my sinful nature. For I have the desire to do what is good, but I cannot carry it out* (Romans 7:18).

Do we really believe these verses? In order to properly understand the plot of David and Bathsheba, we must. In the latter bookend, Paul did not say, *I will not carry it out,* but rather, *I cannot carry it out.* Our failure to conform to God's moral code is not so much a matter of the will as it is a matter of ability. Our wills are ensnared in a web of total depravity that every man inherits at birth. David and Bathsheba were by no means immune to the corrosive effects of that sin-nature. Neither were they immune to the consequences of sin, as we shall see. We ought not to be surprised that a man, regenerated by the power of God's saving Grace, was still capable of engaging in incredible acts of evil. In his burning lust for Bathsheba, David broke all fellowship with God. He disregarded the power of God's mighty victories over his enemies and abandoned sweet communion with the Spirit. He shed his own conscience and made moral choices that would eventually bankrupt the abundance of his own soul for the rest of his life. He did this for one fleeting moment of indulgence in the lusts of his fallen flesh. Was it worth it?

We have looked at the lives of Tamar, Rahab and Ruth in fairly graphic detail. As we visit Bathsheba, we will discover that she may have been the most controversial of all of our Midwives of the Messiah. In light of the two realities above, let us examine what happened when a beautiful woman took a bath in full view of a voyeur king. With Grace in mind, let's look at her unique circumstances.

The record in 1 Samuel tells us that David saw this woman taking a bath at a time of the day when he should have been tending to the duties of war. Seeing her beauty, he craved a physical relationship with her—and the plot thickened. There was a problem—she was married to a very loyal soldier in David's own army who was willing to sacrifice his own life for his king and, ironically, ended up doing so. David abused his God-given power and fell prey to adultery and murder. With this horrific abuse of power, it is easier to focus more on David and overlook the devastation that erupted in Bathsheba's life. We need to have a better understanding of Bathsheba's character, what made her tick, and how she became a Midwife of the Messiah.

Rearing its ugly head in this drama is the sin of pride which has always been at the heart of man's ageless penchant for sin. *Pride goes before destruction, a haughty spirit before a fall* (Proverbs 16:18). We are most vulnerable to moral failure in our spiritual journey either at the onset of, or in the wake of, some great spiritual victory. David and his army had almost completely defeated the enemy as winter set in. The lopsided victory boasted of staggering enemy losses—40,000 soldiers and nearly 7,000 charioteers killed. David returned home for the winter break from this incredible victory to the praise and adulation of his people. As spring approached, the army prepared for one last assault on the remaining enemy stronghold with victory once again assured. David had to be feeling pretty good about himself and the seeming preeminence of his kingdom.

With a sudden rush of self-confidence, and in a moment of exuberance David lowered his spiritual guard. Bathsheba and her husband Uriah lived very close to David. Uriah is recorded as one of David's "Thirty Mighty Men" and was likely an officer of some rank. As such, he would have been invited to David's palace for certain social occasions. David attempted to get Uriah drunk during one such visit, as we shall see. At the time of our story, Uriah was out of town attending to his military responsibilities.

The legendary King David was on the fast track toward moral catastrophe with the danger signs and the combustible materials all in place. The only thing needed was a spark to ignite this moral forest fire. Idleness, the lust of the eyes and a healthy dose of pride served this purpose well.

"In the spring, at a time when kings go off to war, David sent Joab out with the king's men and the whole Israelite army. They destroyed the Ammonites and besieged Rabbah. But David remained in Jerusalem. One evening David got up from his bed and walked around on the roof of the palace. From the roof he saw a woman bathing. The woman was very beautiful..." (2 Samuel 11:1-2)

It was the time of the year when Israel's military campaign against the Ammonites was about to resume. After their armies had been well-rested and re-supplied during the winter, warrior-kings routinely planned to return to the battlefield–but not David. Instead of providing upfront personal leadership for his men, *David remained in Jerusalem.* Only one generation later, David's son, Solomon, would assemble a treasure trove of wisdom in the pages of the Proverbs. There, he warned his own son not to even walk in the direction of sinful temptation (Proverbs 5:7-8). Adultery and its devastating consequences was one of the sins he had in mind as he watched a young man, *with idle hands*, go out looking for trouble and quickly find it (Proverbs 7:6-23). Solomon may well have had his own father in mind as he penned those very words!"

The woman was very beautiful (2 Samuel 11:2). Bathsheba possessed extraordinary physical beauty. Flavius Josephus, a first century Jewish historian, commented on Bathsheba's great beauty as well as Uriah's reputation as a skilled warrior. Their status in Israel and the historian's complimentary description of them gives us the picture of a couple who were loyal to each other and a credit to their king. They certainly did not deserve to have their loyalty rewarded with treachery.

Homes in Jerusalem at that time were constructed using a four-pillar configuration, allowing them to rise to two or more stories high. Many of the houses included flat roofs intended for use as normal living space during spring and summer weather, as well as for entertaining friends, eating meals, sleeping and, yes—with minimal worries about privacy–even bathing. The king's quarters, however, were significantly taller than any of the surrounding homes. It afforded a bird's-eye view for miles around and, of course, a perfect line of sight to dozens of local rooftops—ample opportunity for invasion of privacy for anyone so inclined. David was so inclined.

And David sent someone to find out about her. The man said, "Isn't this Bathsheba, the daughter of Eliam and the wife of Uriah the Hittite?" Then David sent messengers to get her. She came to him, and he slept with her. (She had purified herself from her uncleanness.) Then she went back home. (2 Samuel 11:3-4)

The passage above and those that follow give us the progression of events that led to David's perverted rationale for having Uriah killed. He first sent a spy to confirm the identity of this fascinating woman. The report came back that she was indeed the wife of Uriah the Hittite. Shockingly, this didn't bother or deter David at all. Imagine Bathsheba's state of mind when she was summoned before the king. She had no idea what awaited her. Perhaps there was an urgent message concerning her husband—after all, he was an obedient soldier in harm's way. Or, maybe the king had an important assignment for her. Whatever she was thinking, there is nothing to indicate that she went to the palace with the purpose of seducing David. Her response to the summons was to immediately obey the authority structure over her. She may well have been subdued by the intimidating powers of the king. Disobedience was an offense that could bring severe punishment. In spite of all the warning signs, David blindly followed his lust and sent his men to bring Bathsheba—forcibly, if necessary—into the palace. He then slept with her and sent her away. Mission accomplished. No apparent consequences. It is time to move on.

The mention of her ceremonial cleansing is noteworthy—*She had purified herself from her uncleanness.* This *was* totally consistent with Jewish ceremonial hygienic practices. Before David's men took her, she was doing what she was supposed to be doing in anticipation of her husband returning home from war on military leave. Bathsheba's cleansing was completely appropriate and routine. We should be careful not to jump to the conclusion that Bathsheba was a sultry temptress. The greater offense was David's. He took the first steps toward adultery and abused his great power and influence to get what he wanted, even if it involved conspiracy to murder.

In 2 Samuel, chapters 8 through 10, God gives us a summary of the very impressive battles that David and his armies had fought. One by one, his enemies fell by the mighty hand of God and through David's obedience to Him. They even arose two at a time and were soundly defeated. David was a proven leader, a giant-killer [e.g. Goliath] with twenty years of experience. His people were willing to run through brick walls for David. He had an army comprised of the choicest fighting men, territorial possessions of over sixty thousand square miles, an undefeated battle record and a booming economy.

He presided over a vast and developing infrastructure, a healthy treasury, a stellar cabinet, a strong national defense and a designer home with an "enviable" view. He had plans on the drawing board for an elaborate and ornate temple and a clear moral mandate from God to lead His people. What more could possibly be said in admiration of one man? There stood the king of Israel who had everything, gazing down from his balcony and lusting after a married woman, and then abusing his power to have sex with her. Joab and the Israelite army were off to war while David slept in. His eyes should have been on the Ammonites, but instead, they were on Bathsheba.

There is a slippery slope of moral failure that is further greased when we find ourselves where we ought not to be, and doing things we ought not to be doing. It is during those moments of deep spiritual vulnerability that we tend to forget the great past victories God has given. It is when our guard is down that the enemy strikes. Every claim God made upon David, every obligation of the high office, and all the fences that Divine Mercy had built to protect him, were ruthlessly trampled underfoot by the fiery lusts now burning within him. What followed was a cascade of consequences that David had never anticipated—but should have!

The woman conceived and sent word to David, saying, "I am pregnant." (2 Samuel 11:5)

When she realized she was pregnant, new fears set in: "What will my husband say? What will his family do? What will happen to this baby?" Her life was sliding down that slippery slope. Josephus raised the possibility that the reason Bathsheba told David she was pregnant was to warn him of possible retribution. They both knew that the law of the land demanded the death penalty for the act of adultery, regardless of whether or not she had consented. It would be very interesting, but not hard, to speculate whether the death penalty would have actually been imposed on the king, or whether the female victim alone would have become the scapegoat.

Bathsheba was the victim of a man whose God-given power had gone to his head. David proudly reasoned that, since he had been given everything by the hand of God, he was entitled to anything he desired. However, David was soon to learn that the concept of selfish entitlement was foreign to God. In desperation, he had to find a way to cover up his sin. Steeped in a moral abyss, he devised a plan to make it appear as though the unborn child belonged to Uriah. David ordered Joab to send Uriah home from the front for a little exercise in royal deception. He was even so bold as to pretend he was interested in the welfare of his men and the progress of the war:

So David sent this word to Joab: "Send me Uriah the Hittite." And Joab sent him to David. When Uriah came to him, David asked him how Joab was, how the soldiers were and how the war was going. Then David said to Uriah, "Go down to your house and wash your feet." So Uriah left the palace, and a gift from the king was sent after him. But Uriah slept at the entrance to the palace with all his master's servants and did not go down to his house. When David was told, "Uriah did not go home," he asked him, "Haven't you just come from a distance? Why didn't you go home?" (2 Samuel 11:6-10)

His scheme did not work. David's evil intentions came face to face with Uriah's integrity and sense of honor. This *man after God's own heart* should have been put to shame—if he was even capable of feeling shame at this juncture.

Uriah said to David, "The ark and Israel and Judah are staying in tents, and my master Joab and my lord's men are camped in the open fields. How could I go to my house to eat and drink and lie with my wife? As surely as you live, I will not do such a thing!" (2 Samuel 11:11)

Uriah was a dedicated, professional soldier who stood by his oath of allegiance to his duty and to his men. In this time of war Uriah refused to enjoy the comforts of home, including physical intimacy with his own wife, while his troops endured harsh conditions in the field. Time for Plan B:

Then David said to him, "Stay here one more day, and tomorrow I will send you back." So Uriah remained in Jerusalem that day and the next. At David's invitation, he ate and drank with him, and David made him drunk. But in the evening Uriah went out to sleep on his mat among his master's servants; he did not go home. (2 Samuel 11:12-13)

David invited Uriah to spend the night in the royal palace. His invitation was not a friendly act of hospitality—it was a scheme to get Uriah drunk. David reasoned that, if inebriated, Uriah would lose his compulsion to continue his sexual fast while his loyal comrades were still in harm's way. In a drunken stupor, perhaps Uriah would return to his home, have a sexual relationship with his wife, and proudly believe that the child was his own. Uriah did not return home, so Plan B was in trouble—that is, until David decided that Uriah had to be eliminated before David could be exposed as the child's father. The palace staff likely knew what their king was up to. Is it possible that Uriah suspected what was going on as well and refused to be a party to this great sin? Perhaps! It was time for Plan C.

David plotted with Joab, his military commander, and ordered him to send Uriah to the front lines where the fighting was fiercest. When the enemy stormed their position, Joab pulled back and deserted Uriah since David made it clear to Joab that Uriah must die. The plan worked, and in the process not only did Uriah die, but some of David's best men paid the ultimate price for David's laziness and lust (2 Samuel 11:14-21).

David dodged a bullet. His little secret was safe, or so he thought. He later took Bathsheba for his wife (2 Samuel 11:27) even though their marriage had no moral standing since David stole her from Uriah. The Scripture is silent as to how agreeable Bathsheba initially was to this turn of events. David, however, was the king—he could do anything he pleased. There is no suggestion anywhere that Bathsheba ever lost her love for Uriah. She married David but she belonged to Uriah. In the genealogy of Jesus, it reads *David was the father of Solomon, whose mother had been Uriah's wife* (Matthew

1:6). Wow! This historic scandal is right there for all to see. Later in his life, as David looked back at these events and his shameful behavior before God and his loyal subjects, he wrote in Psalm 51:3, *for I know my transgressions, and my sin is always before me.* How true—for all of us.

David, not unlike other kings, had harems and numerous wives, mainly political in nature. While in Hebron, David had several wives and concubines and fathered many children by them (1 Chronicles 1:9 and 3:1-9), even though God never commanded or condoned polygamy. Although socially and politically it may have been advantageous for David to build his empire through political marriages, God never directed him to do so. In fact, the qualifications for becoming a king included this: *He must not take many wives, or his heart will be led astray* (Deuteronomy 17:17).

The Biblical record of the polygamous practices of great men such as Jacob and Solomon is filled with the aftermath of its consequences. Rape, incest and all manner of horrors plagued these men and infected their legacies after them. Likewise, this is true of David as we will see. All of the consequences for David's bad choices also affected Bathsheba directly. Imagine the pain she had to live with.

The amazing irony of this story is that, in spite of all of David's moral failures, God redeemed him and called him a man after His own heart. David accumulated great power, wealth and prestige. At the time of these events, David was middle-aged. He had surely been around the block a few times and had been carried by the Grace of his God over many miraculous miles. He was victorious in battle. He had remained faithful to Saul who sought to kill him. He stood on mountaintops of great courage and conviction, and walked through valleys of personal hell while surrounded by God's protective love. What happened to him? He had grown sons who had to witness a dad out of control. He was the king of the most powerful nation on earth—what an example to his flock. After his murderous deed, his military leaders had to be thinking, "What's going to happen to my wife–or to me, for that matter—while I'm away?" David had lost all dignity and respect.

David's journey toward repentance and restoration began with a visit from Nathan the Prophet who told him this parable:

The Lord sent Nathan to David. When he came to him, he said, "There were two men in a certain town, one rich and the other poor. The rich man had a very large number of sheep and cattle, but the poor man had nothing except one little ewe lamb he had bought. He raised it, and it grew up with him and his children. It shared his food, drank from his cup and even slept in his arms. It was like a daughter to him. "Now a traveler came to the rich man, but the rich man refrained from taking one of his own sheep or cattle to prepare a meal for the traveler who had come to him. Instead, he took the ewe lamb that belonged to the poor man and prepared it for the one who had come to him." David burned with anger against the man and said to Nathan, "As surely as the Lord lives, the man who did this deserves to die! He must pay for that lamb four times over, because he did such a thing and had no pity." Then Nathan said to David, "You are the man!" (2 Samuel 12:1-7a)

The flushed face and burning chest pains that must have gripped David at the dramatic moment of those words, *you are the man* paled in significance to what followed—a not-so-user-friendly sermon:

This is what the Lord, the God of Israel, says: 'I anointed you king over Israel, and I delivered you from the hand of Saul. I gave your master's house to you, and your master's wives into your arms. I gave you the house of Israel and Judah. And if all this had been too little, I would have given you even more. Why did you despise the word of the Lord by doing what is evil in his eyes? You struck down Uriah the Hittite with the sword and took his wife to be your own. You killed him with the sword of the Ammonites. Now, therefore, the sword will never depart from your house, because you despised me and took the wife of Uriah the Hittite to be your own.' "This is what the Lord says: 'Out of your own house-

hold I am going to bring calamity upon you. Before your very eyes I will take your wives and give them to one who is close to you, and he will lie with your wives in broad daylight. You did it in secret, but I will do this thing in broad daylight before all Israel.'" Then David said to Nathan, "I have sinned against the Lord." Nathan replied, "The Lord has taken away your sin. You are not going to die. But because by doing this you have made the enemies of the Lord show utter contempt, the son born to you will die." (2 Samuel 12:7b-14)

Talk about a sermon with some bite to it! Perhaps these thoughts rushed through David's head: "Nathan is a real irritating guy to have around. Does he not have anything better to do than to pick on me? And who does he think he is anyway? I am the king. How dare he talk to me this way?" That is not what happened. Instead, God used Nathan in his calling as a Prophet to scorch David's conscience and opened for him a direct channel for the voice of God to be heard. David reeled with sorrow as he imagined the consequences. He was going to lose a child. What would he tell Bathsheba, whom he loved and who knew nothing of this punishment to come? How could he tell her that her baby was going to die because of him? A scene of unimaginable pain and brokenness followed.

After Nathan had gone home, the Lord struck the child that Uriah's wife had borne to David, and he became ill. David pleaded with God for the child. He fasted and went into his house and spent the nights lying on the ground. The elders of his household stood beside him to get him up from the ground, but he refused, and he would not eat any food with them. On the seventh day the child died. David's servants were afraid to tell him that the child was dead, for they thought, "While the child was still living, we spoke to David but he would not listen to us. How can we tell him the child is dead? He may do something desperate." David noticed that his servants were whispering among themselves and he realized the child was dead. "Is the child dead?" he asked. "Yes," they replied, "he is dead." (2 Samuel 12:15-19)

David spent seven days lying face down on the ground in anguish and refused to eat. He physically and emotionally fell apart before his servants' very eyes. In spite of David's pleading for God to spare the child, the baby fell grievously ill. After seven tortuous days, the little baby died. His servants delayed telling David the bad news for fear he would commit suicide. Josephus records that David's pleas and bitter mourning during that time were, in great part, due to his love for Bathsheba as well as for the young boy.

Then David got up from the ground. After he had washed, put on lotions and changed his clothes, he went into the house of the Lord and worshiped. Then he went to his own house, and at his request they served him food, and he ate. His servants asked him, "Why are you acting this way? While the child was alive, you fasted and wept, but now that the child is dead, you get up and eat!" He answered, "While the child was still alive, I fasted and wept. I thought, 'Who knows? The Lord may be gracious to me and let the child live.' But now that he is dead, why should I fast? Can I bring him back again? I will go to him, but he will not return to me." (2 Samuel 12:20-23)

David made a wise choice to submit himself to the will of God. He also made a very interesting statement that is one of the earliest references in the Old Testament to the believer's Hope of eternal life: *why should I fast? Can I bring him back again? <u>I will go to him</u>, but he will not return to me* (2 Samuel 12:23; emphasis mine).

How beautifully reminiscent of similar words of hope David penned:

...and I will dwell in the house of the Lord forever. (Psalm 23:6)

The choice he made corresponds to that point in time when God began to call him *a man after His own heart*. God blessed David's repentance with a more positive event that followed: *Then David comforted his wife Bathsheba, and he went to her and lay with her. She gave birth to a son and they named him* Solomon (2 Samuel 12:24; emphasis mine).

He mustered enough of a conscience to look with compassion on Bathsheba for the pain he caused her in the loss of the first child she bore. The death of this child marked a pivotal point in David's journey of repentance and renewal. David was at the proverbial fork in the road where he had to make a choice. He could continue in his pride and denial or turn to the God who stood patiently waiting to forgive.

The name Solomon or Jedidiah means "beloved of the Lord." *Because the Lord loved him, he sent word through Nathan the prophet to name him Jedidiah* (2 Samuel 12:25). David bore the curse of his restless home in a variety of ways, such as the betrayal by his own son, Absalom, and the many, many wars David would have to fight. He yearned for peace when there was no peace. He would never see that great Temple built, for God stripped him of that privilege.

If we stare into the mirror of our own souls, we will certainly see the images of King David as well as the reluctant and infamous housewife, Bathsheba, who also had to bear the pain as well as experience the redemption that followed in the wake of David's sin.

Was Bathsheba merely another woman in a long line of sexual conquests on the part of a morally bankrupt king? Is she simply an afterthought in this powerful story of lust, murder and betrayal, upstaged by the immoral antics of King David, *or* did God put her in this place and at this time to fulfill an eternal plan He was working out behind the scenes? More specifically, *what lessons can we learn from Bathsheba's story?*

The story of Bathsheba testifies to the fact that the promises God makes in heaven cannot be vetoed by the sinful acts of man. Her story is a tragedy that gives way to redemption. Through Nathan the Prophet, God extended to David and Bathsheba the Covenant of Grace, an irrevocable promise of what God planned to do with them and their household:

"When your days are over and you rest with your fathers, I will raise up your offspring to succeed you, who will come from your own body, and I will establish his kingdom... Your house and your kingdom will endure forever before me; your throne will be established forever." (2 Samuel 7:12&17)

Bathsheba played a key role, not only in giving birth to Solomon, but also in frustrating Satan's ongoing plan to sabotage the advent of the Messiah. When David was old and bedridden, a plot to usurp his kingdom arose:

Now Adonijah, whose mother was Haggith, put himself forward and said, "I will be king." So he got chariots and horses ready, with fifty men to run ahead of him. (His father had never interfered with him by asking, "Why do you behave as you do?" He was also very handsome and was born next after Absalom.) Adonijah conferred with Joab son of Zeruiah and with Abiathar the priest and they gave him their support. But Zadok the priest, Benaiah son of Jehoiada, Nathan the prophet, Shimei and Rei and David's special guard did not join Adonijah. (1 Kings 1:5-8)

Who was Adonijah? David had many, many children by his many, many wives. When David lived in Hebron, he fathered four sons. By the time of David's impending death, all of them were dead except Adonijah. He was the fourth and the oldest surviving of David's sons born there (2 Sam. 3:2-5). Adonijah attempted to usurp David's (and God's) right to name the next king. Adonijah conspired with Joab and Abiathar, two men who had a longstanding history with David. Joab was the commander of David's armies. Years before, Abiathar had fled to David for protection from the wrath of then King Saul. David took him in and protected him. In a surprising reversal of loyalty, these men joined Adonijah's plot. Some friends!

Adonijah was a handsome man who was never told "no" as a boy. Like David's other notorious and rebellious son, Absalom, Adonijah was in part the product of paternal negligence and indulgence. David never held him accountable for his actions and rarely disciplined him. One would expect that the fruit of such horrible parenting skills would come back to haunt David—and it did. Adonijah threw a party and invited only his Judean "yes men." Noticeably absent were the leading men of David's Israel. Adonijah knew that they would have counseled him differently—they would have told him "no." He did not invite Nathan the Prophet or David's Mighty Men—the Special Forces. Adonijah, in essence, anointed himself as the new king.

Then Nathan asked Bathsheba, Solomon's mother, "Have you not heard that Adonijah, the son of Haggith, has become king without our lord David's knowing it? Now then, let me advise you how you can save your own life and the life of your son Solomon. Go in to King David and say to him, 'My lord the king, did you not swear to me your servant: "Surely Solomon your son shall be king after me, and he will sit on my throne"? Why then has Adonijah become king?' While you are still there talking to the king, I will come in and confirm what you have said." So Bathsheba went to see the aged king in his room, where Abishag the Shunammite was attending him. (1 Kings 1:11-15)

Bathsheba and Nathan informed David of Adonijah's plot. David remembered God's promise concerning Solomon delivered to him years before by Nathan the Prophet.[1] The Messianic birth line was reconfirmed by David's response to Bathsheba.

I will surely carry out today what I swore to you by the Lord, the God of Israel: Solomon your son shall be king after me, and he will sit on my throne in my place." (1 Kings 1:30; emphasis mine)

Bathsheba and Nathan foiled the plot to lock Solomon out of succession to the throne and took decisive action to inform King David who then ordered a very public and festive coronation of Solomon. So loud was the celebration that when Adonijah heard it he ran into the holy place and clung to the horns of the altar for asylum.[2] Adonijah successfully begged Solomon for mercy, which was short-lived. He made another effort to subvert Solomon's reign and that cost him his life.[3]

The story of Bathsheba teaches us that our dire circumstances can become a platform to glorify God. Bathsheba provided a loving atmosphere in her home for her son, Solomon, and her husband, David, despite the constant demands of war that disrupted their lives. There is nothing to indicate that David was any better a father to Solomon than he was to Adonijah. For years, Bathsheba faithfully raised Solomon from boyhood to manhood as they came to share a very special bond. Solomon greatly respected his mother and did not mind demonstrating it publicly (1 Kings 2:19). We may safely assume that Bathsheba imparted to her son much of the wisdom he was known to possess.[4]

For many years, Bathsheba had to live with a man of war as her husband. She raised Solomon in an environment of sibling rivalry and strife. Her husband struggled with spiritual depression and soulful regret as he mourned over his sin. He wrote Psalm 51 for the purpose of confessing the pain he caused by his many wrong moral choices. *O, that our own hearts would be so broken over our sins as was David's.* He brought shame and dishonor upon himself, his family, his nation and his God. Bathsheba had to live with this emotional time bomb every day of her life with David.

The core value of Solomon's Book of the Proverbs is the fear of God. Where did Solomon learn this principle? Who taught Solomon how to fear God? His parents did, but Bathsheba was Solomon's instructor and disciplinarian. She had a tough life that began with that innocent roof-top bath. She was victimized by an out-of-control king. She lost her first husband to a sinister plot devised by her second husband. She delivered a baby and God took him away as a punishment for her husband's sin. She lived with a man who battled spiritual depression. She was surrounded by David's many wives and their offspring vying for power and position. Wars raging inside and outside her home set the tone for a life of relentless strife.

Consider this—Adonijah's mother was Haggith, who appeared on the pages of the Bible out of nowhere and disappeared just as quickly. She gave birth to a pretender who was eventually executed for treason. Solomon's mother was Bathsheba, a woman who found her place in the genealogy of the Messiah. She gave birth to a boy who would become the most powerful man in the world revered for his legendary wisdom.

Was Bathsheba a temptress, a victim or something else? Her legacy is much more positive and enduring than Bathsheba herself could ever have imagined. In spite of all that has transpired in their story, this was the only hope David and Bathsheba could cling to—that God is sovereign and they could trust Him. Even in the face of our own seemingly hopeless circumstances, our God is sovereign and *we* can trust Him.

Catapulted from obscurity into the spotlight of history, this strong but reluctant heroine stands silently in the shadows beside that manger in Bethlehem and gazes upon it with a knowing smile on her face. At the long-awaited birth of Messiah, the One Who would come through the loins of David and through Bathsheba's own son Solomon; we can almost hear our weary Midwife whisper, "*Now* it all makes sense!"

---

[1]David's promise to Solomon that he would inherit the throne is recorded in 1 Chronicles 22:6-10.

[2] This was consistent with a common Near Eastern belief that, if a fugitive sought refuge in and clung to a holy place, he would be spared from the wrath of the one who sought to kill him. This concept was similar to the broader system of protections introduced by Moses, under God's direction, when he established "Cities of Refuge" after the Hebrews entered the Promised Land (Numbers 35:6-15).

[3] Compare 1 Kings 2:13-25 with 2 Samuel 16:20-22.

[4] The ramifications of David's sin would eventually become the very root of moral failure in his son, Solomon (2 Kings 11:1-8). Throughout the final years of David's reign, the greatest king in all of Israel's history bore the haunting memories and deep conviction of past sins that were ever before him.

In the story of Mary, a frightened teenager and our fifth Midwife of the Messiah, we will snap a picture of unparalleled humility, faith and absolute submission to the will of God. Mary's song of worship about her newborn Savior and Son is the perfect culmination of the many contributions made by the other four Midwives of the Messiah.

Chapter 5: Mary

One of the most beautiful and peaceful songs you will ever hear is *Ave Maria*. The first half of this song contains intense doctrine and is pregnant with meaning. Many renditions of this classic song have been sung, played, and spoken in nearly every modern language in addition to the original Latin. The opening words of this moving masterpiece read as follows:

> *Áve María, grátia pléna, Dóminus técum. Benedícta tu in muliéribus, et benedíctus frúctus véntris túi, Iésus.*

Translated, it reads, *Hail Mary, full of grace, the Lord is with thee. Blessed art thou amongst women and blessed is the fruit of thy womb, Jesus.*

These words were first sung by the angel Gabriel over two thousand years ago to a Godly young woman, a virgin who would literally become the sole human conduit between our sovereign God in Heaven and His most dramatic physical invasion of human history.

Within many cultural settings around the world, Christmas is the most anticipated and beloved holiday of the year. Traditionally, on this one special day, battlefields fall silent, hopes and dreams are born and fractured relationships are healed. It is a time when people focus on happiness, family, food, fellowship and optimistic plans. Parents desperately begin the age-old search for that one special toy that Junior simply "cannot live without." Years ago, competing adult toy hunters would practically kill for the last Cabbage Patch doll on the shelf. Today's children have replaced "visions of sugar plums" with expectations of Wii video games and WebKinz "computer-interactive" plush animals. Since every passing year seems to bring us more crises and complexities in current events and personal relationships, we can hardly blame people for looking forward to a brief time-out on the calendar when worries can be temporarily laid aside while dreams of hope and peace occupy their hearts.

The Christmas drama exhibits the characteristics of innocence and simplicity—the grand love story of the young couple, Joseph and Mary, and the breathtaking miracle that God worked through them. Mary was probably a teenager. Her family lived on the lower rungs of the social and economic ladder. She was formally engaged to a local craftsman, Joseph, when her life took a dramatic turn. Engagement was considered as legally binding as marriage. During the engagement period, a sexual relationship was treated as adultery. The Old Testament penalty of stoning for the sin of adultery was still on the books, but was not consistently enforced at that time. Nonetheless, the shame of a scandalous pregnancy would ruin the lives of any couple found in this predicament. When God invaded the relationship of Mary and Joseph, they found themselves in precisely this predicament.

Mary's story begins with a frightening encounter with a messenger from God:

In [Elizabeth's] sixth month, God sent the angel Gabriel to Nazareth, a town in Galilee, to a virgin pledged to be married to a man named Joseph, a descendant of David. The virgin's name was Mary. The angel went to her and said, "Greetings, you who are highly favored! The Lord is with you." Mary was greatly troubled at his words and wondered what kind of greeting this might be. But the angel said to her, "Do not be afraid, Mary, you have found favor with God. You will be with child and give birth to a son, and you are to give him the name Jesus. He will be great and will be called the Son of the Most High. The Lord God will give him the throne of his father David and he will reign over the house of Jacob forever; his kingdom will never end." (Luke 1:26-33)

With the earth-shaking implications of the above verses in mind, I want to emphasize the fundamental premise upon which this book rests and upon which the very meaning of the Incarnation itself depends:

The virgin birth declares the Deity of Jesus, the infinite God-Man. The virgin birth was necessary for several reasons. First, Jesus is pre-existent, that is, He existed from the beginning. He had no creator since He *is* the Creator. His birth merely moved Him from eternity into time, from the invisible world into the visible world. *In the beginning was the Word, and the Word was with God, and the Word was God* (John 1:1). Who is this *Word?* John answers this question—*The Word became flesh and made his dwelling among us. We have seen his glory, the glory of the One and Only, who came from the Father, full of grace and truth* (John 1:14).[1] When Jesus came into the world, He was not a newly created individual such as we are, but was rather the eternal Son of God. To be born into this world of a virgin required a Divine miracle. This is exactly what the Gospels record.

Second, Jesus had to be born of a virgin since He could not be stained with the sin nature of man. If He had been born by the sexual union between a man and a woman, then Jesus would have been merely a man and not the infinite God-Man. A basic premise of the New Testament is that from the day He was born until the day He went to the cross, Jesus was without sin. On the Old Testament feast Day of Atonement, the lamb that was to be sacrificed had to be flawless. This was the archetype that pointed to the Lord Jesus Christ. In order to be our perfect sacrifice, He had to be flawless and without blemish. That is, the Messiah had to be without sin. Since our race is contaminated with sin, a miraculous entrance into the world would be required, hence the virgin birth.

Third, if Jesus' biological father was Joseph, He would not have been able to claim the legal right to the throne of

David. Remember, the Messiah must be a descendant of David. In the genealogy of Jesus, Matthew tells us that, although Joseph was indeed a descendant of David, he also came from the line of Jechoniah (Matthew 1:12-16).[2] However, Jechoniah was cursed:

Is this man Jehoiachin a despised, broken pot, an object no one wants? Why will he and his children be hurled out, cast into a land they do not know? O land, land, land, hear the word of the Lord! This is what the Lord says: "Record this man as if childless, a man who will not prosper in his lifetime, for none of his offspring will prosper, none will sit on the throne of David or rule anymore in Judah." (Jeremiah 22:28-30)

According to this Scripture, there could be no king in Israel who was from the line of King Jeconiah. Apart from the virgin birth, Jesus would have been born of the cursed lineage and not a rightful heir to the throne of David. Thus, He would not have any claim to being the Messiah.[3]

The virgin birth of Christ was a necessary historical fact when one considers all the data. Any deviation from this firm assertion undermines the credibility and central message of the Bible itself. In order to be a Christian, one must embrace the child of Mary in the manger as the very Creator God of the universe. Our salvation is inseparably tied to His identity as the Son of God. If Jesus had been conceived through a normal sexual union between Mary and Joseph, He would merely have been another sinful man and not the infinite God-Man. If Christ was nothing more than a sinful man, His ability to save would be nonexistent. His death on the cross would be a meaningless exercise of one morally-polluted sinner dying for another. There could be no atonement in that. Within the Christmas story, the virgin birth in particular is so vital to understanding the nature of God and our relationship to him.

Although Jesus is fully man, He is also fully God. The entire body of evidence upon which we hang our claim of Christ's Deity centers on the clear Biblical claim of His virgin birth. Christ was conceived in the womb of the Virgin Mary and clothed in human flesh in order to be fully man, but He was conceived by the Holy Spirit so that He would be fully God. Everything that God ever was, is or will be is wrapped up in the person and character of Jesus Christ. He is not merely one in a long line of prophetic figures; He is the Creator-God of the universe who stepped into a human body so that He could die on a cross to provide salvation for His people. Every modern-day cult also understands the implications of this and makes the virgin birth the center of their attacks on Christianity. Discredit the virgin birth and you have discredited and dismissed all of Christianity. The Bible then becomes a collection of entertaining, but also suspect, bedtime stories—and we are forever lost in our sins. My question to the skeptic is, "Who, then, is this Jesus?" How could a mere man live a perfect life? How could a mere man rise from the dead, raise others from the dead, walk on water or feed the thousands? Why do these skeptics even bother to celebrate Christmas?

The angel Gabriel's announcement left Mary frightened and confused. She knew she was a virgin. She shared the news with Joseph, including the details of her "chat" with the heavenly visitor. One can only imagine Joseph's own confusion, disbelief and certain anger. After all, he loved Mary and wanted to spend the rest of his life with her. They were nearly married. Her father promised her to Joseph in purity and the wedding date was set. The interfamily dowry negotiations had been settled—and then she made this shocking announcement. Joseph now faced two options: expose her as unfaithful or divorce her quietly to avoid the shame. For him, there would be no other human resolutions to this embarrassing dilemma. Can you imagine how Mary could have ever expected Joseph to believe her? Her story was completely implausible. Most likely, Joseph wondered about her mental and emotional state. He assumed she had already been unfaithful to him.

One way existed for this situation to be resolved—miraculously. Joseph was visited by an angel in a dream. The angel assured him that Mary's story was true. In the following passage, notice that the word "husband" is used to describe Joseph even though he and Mary are "only" engaged:

Because Joseph her husband was a righteous man and did not want to expose her to public disgrace, he had in mind to divorce her quietly. But after he had considered this, an angel of the Lord appeared to him in a dream and said, "Joseph son of David, do not be afraid to take Mary home as your wife, because what is conceived in her is from the Holy Spirit.[4] *She will give birth to a son, and you are to give him the name Jesus, because he will save his people from their sins."* (Matthew 1:19-21)

Joseph's faith and character was impressive. He readily accepted God's miraculous plan and lovingly took Mary back. Mary decided to share her fantastic news with her dear relative, Elizabeth, who lived nearby in the hill country of Judea. Her visit was not an impulsive decision but rather a direct result of the message given to her by the angel: *Even Elizabeth your relative is going to have a child in her old age, and she who was said to be barren is in her sixth month. For nothing is impossible with God* (Luke 1:36).

Elizabeth's pregnancy had begun six months earlier than Mary's. Mary had to know of Elizabeth's barrenness and was all the more excited about "comparing notes" with her older and very pregnant cousin. A late-life pregnancy was a surprise for Elizabeth and her priest husband, Zechariah—one more example of a perfectly timed puzzle piece in God's planned mosaic. The Holy Spirit miraculously deposited His Seed, the promised *Seed of the Woman* (Genesis 3:15), into Mary's womb. The curtain was about to rise for the final act in this cosmic drama. The previous preparatory scenes had already been played out by our other four Midwives. John the Baptizer, Jesus' forerunner by six months, would be the one privileged with pulling back that final curtain as he announced the coming of the Messiah to a lost world. Every young Jewess dreamed of being the one through whom the Messiah would come. Mary would live out that dream, for nothing is impossible with God.

When Mary arrived at Elizabeth's home, they happily greeted each other and, as their eyes met, the Scripture says that the baby in Elizabeth's womb "leaped for joy." Even from the womb, there was worshipful recognition and John the Baptist was, in essence, bowing before the Christ Child. Elizabeth too, realized she was suddenly standing in the presence of the Messiah and immediately uttered words that could be considered her own "hymn" of joy:

When Elizabeth heard Mary's greeting, the baby leaped in her womb, and Elizabeth was filled with the Holy Spirit. In a loud voice she exclaimed: "Blessed are you among women, and blessed is the child you will bear! But why am I so favored, that the mother of my Lord should come to me? As soon as the sound of your greeting reached my ears, the baby in my womb leaped for joy. Blessed is she who has believed that what the Lord has said to her will be accomplished!" (Luke 1:41-45)

If Mary had any lingering doubts or fears, she laid them aside when she heard Elizabeth's words confirming everything the angel had told her—before Mary even had a chance to announce that she was pregnant. It was now clear to Mary that God had directed her journey to visit Elizabeth. With her spirit soaring, Mary could no longer contain the praise and gratitude that was welling up inside her. She burst out in a song, one of the many such songs that underscored the majesty and joy of the birth of Christ, *The Magnificat*. When we read Luke's account of the events surrounding the birth of Jesus, we hear the heavenly music of Christmas—the original Christmas Carols. We are permitted to eavesdrop on the very first "worship service" offered by human beings to Christ in person while He was on earth.

A pregnant virgin! An old woman six months pregnant! A leaping baby in the womb! What else could possibly make this drama any more exciting? The Old Testament ended with John's arrival and the New Testament began with Christ's arrival. Now, with our other faith-heroines, Mary joined hands to complete the Covenant promise and became the last of the five Midwives of the Messiah. The final plank was laid in the bridge that carried us from the promise God made to the devil—that the *Seed of the Woman* would crush his head—to the birth of that Seed. Mary was pregnant with the promise of God to a fallen race. Following Elizabeth, Mary spoke. Remember, this is very likely the voice of a teenager. Mary's song of praise in these verses traditionally has been called *The Magnificat*, a title derived from the opening word, *Magnificat* —meaning *to glorify*. The Magnificat is the first of three hymns in Luke, chapters one and two, the others being the *Benedictus* (1:68–79) and the *Nunc Dimittis* (2:29–32).

Mary's hymn of praise (the Magnificat) follows the common form of Psalms of Thanksgiving, which begin by thanking God and then expressing the reasons for the gratitude. Mary's entire being is caught up in praise to God. The spiritual depth and the prophetic tone of the lyrics only give further evidence of how completely God had gripped her very soul with the power of the Incarnation:

My soul glorifies the Lord
and my spirit rejoices in God my Savior,
for he has been mindful
of the humble state of his servant.
From now on all generations will call me blessed,
for the Mighty One has done great things for me –
Holy is his name.
His mercy extends to those who fear him,
from generation to generation.
He has performed mighty deeds with his arm;
He has scattered those who are proud in their inmost thoughts.
He has brought down rulers from their thrones
but has lifted up the humble.
He has filled the hungry with good things
but has sent the rich away empty.
He has helped his servant Israel,
remembering to be merciful
to Abraham and his descendants forever,
even as he said to our fathers.
(Luke 1:46-55)

Mary added her voice to the angelic choir that was already rehearsing for that dramatic appearance to the shepherds on the hills outside of Bethlehem only nine months later. We can hardly think of Christmas without the melodies and lyrics of these precious songs flooding our hearts.

Mary's song contains two stanzas in this gripping New Testament Psalm. In the first stanza, we listen to *Mary's own experience—Worship at its highest level.* In the second stanza, we hear *Mary's refrain as she celebrates her God.* The innocence and humility of this chosen peasant girl are clearly displayed in this Psalm. Twenty plus centuries later we can still hear a teenager's outpouring of worship and praise to her God—a melody of God's accomplishments in faithfulness to His people.

Do you embrace our God with such innocent, joyful and spontaneous admiration? How would your Magnificat be sung as God works His Grace in your heart? How would your soul express, in language that others could understand, what your God means to you? Mary's world had been rocked and her soul overflowed with submission and trust.

Mary's hymn begins with these words: *My soul glorifies the Lord and my spirit rejoices in God my Savior* (Luke 1:46-47). It is very significant that Mary did not merely say, "*I* glorify the Lord." She spoke more profoundly. The limited vocabulary of a poor young girl was not adequate for expressing, in her own words, all that she was experiencing. At that time, the Holy Spirit came alongside her—according to a promise God would later give to you and me:

...The Spirit helps us in our weakness. We do not know what we ought to pray for, but the Spirit himself intercedes for us with groans that words cannot express. And he who searches our hearts knows the mind of the Spirit, because the Spirit intercedes for the saints in accordance with God's will. (Romans 8:26-27)

The eloquence and power in her words put to rest any doubts as to who was speaking, *For prophesy never had its origin in the will of man, but men spoke from God as they were carried along by the Holy Spirit* (2 Peter 1:21). There is hardly a better example in all of Scripture of someone being *carried along by the Holy Spirit.* Her very soul/spirit, through which the Spirit of God crafted the words of her song, glorified God. Her *soul/spirit,* that is, her entire being that was created in the image and likeness of God—her mind, her emotions, her personality, her character, and her will–could not contain itself. The whole of her being fell down and worshiped God. Her *soul/spirit* welled up within as she openly and unashamedly rejoiced in what God was doing in her life. There was a miracle in progress and she saw it. In one short stanza, this young girl captured what takes many of us a lifetime to express and we still fall short. God gave her utterance as the Spirit carried her.

When we seek to glorify God from the depths of our soul/spirit, we will not quit. We will not give up. We will persevere. We must not limit the mind and heart of God Who desires to do *immeasurably more than all we ask or imagine, according to his power that is at work within us* (Ephesians 3:20). We ought not to even think about making plans for tomorrow unless they, and our heart attitude, are conditioned by the will of God. Submission to the purposes of God is the conduit of Divine blessing.

What we believe about God shapes everything we think, say and do. Our beliefs become the reference point around which we make the minor and major decisions in our lives—what job to take, who to marry, how to raise the children, how to manage the finances and how to respond to the preaching and teaching of the Word of God. What we believe about God determines how we will respond when the lights in our life are turned off and we are engulfed in consuming darkness. Will our *soul/spirit* glorify God?

Mary dedicated herself to the proclamation of God's Truth. The pure joy in her music was contagious for all generations that followed her. Her *soul/spirit*, the fiber of her being, that which was created in the image and likeness of God and that which must be born again, rejoiced in God her Savior. In a glorious panorama of heaven, Revelation, the last book of the Bible, paints an eternal scene of great emotion, joy, celebration, adoration and worship. In one majestic moment, the veil is lifted and we are permitted to eavesdrop on worship in heaven where, in a chorus of antiphonal singing, heaven cannot contain itself. What are they singing?

Holy, Holy, Holy
Is the Lord God Almighty,
Who was, and is, and is to come.
...Praise and glory
And wisdom and thanks and honor
And power and strength
be to our God forever and ever.
Amen

(Revelation 4:8 and 7:12)

The above passage is the perfected *soul/spirit* worship of God. Mary's *soul/spirit* welled up within and she could not contain her praise. As Mary and Elizabeth stood side by side, both pregnant with promise, a snapshot was taken of what it will be like in Glory. However, in our unperfected state, we can seek after holiness, memorize chapters in the Bible, teach and preach all of the mechanics of Christian behavior, and still fall woefully short of what God expects of us. Proper worship is a balance between what we believe and how we express it. Emotional extremism always leads to faulty worship. We can master deep doctrine or revel in shallow emotionalism but still have no *message*. What is the message? Our God sent His Son to die on a cross to purchase a costly salvation for His people. Mary owned that message when she declared *My spirit rejoices in God my Savior.*

The story of Mary teaches us that the Incarnation is inseparably linked to the message of hope that comes from the Cross. The angel Gabriel visited Mary *because there was a message*. The angel comforted and assured Joseph *because there was a message*. Mary hurried off to see Elizabeth *because there was a message*. The angels serenaded the shepherds *because there was a message*. The shepherds departed and told others *because there was a message*. The wise men traveled a great distance *because there was a message*. The Messiah stepped from eternity into history and went to a cross *because there was a message*. And—Jesus built and preserved His Church through two thousand years of persecution and satanic onslaught *because there was* *and is a MESSAGE!* Christ's marching orders concerning that message could not have been clearer:

"All authority in heaven and on earth has been given to me. Therefore go and make disciples of all nations, baptizing them in the name of the Father and of the Son and of the Holy Spirit, and teaching them to obey everything I have commanded you. And surely I am with you always, to the very end of the age." (Matthew 28:18-20)

The story of Mary teaches us that true worship begins with a humble heart that freely admits the need for God's touch and opens channels for us to touch the lives of others. A missionary visited a small, poor Christian congregation near Delhi, India. After he saw the dilapidated chapel where they met, he wrote:

> *"I sat and looked and it was strange. There was a small wooden cross hanging from a thin wire. Behind the cross there was no wall! I could look beyond the cross to what was outside. What I saw was some dirty linen hanging in a bathroom. I could see bedrooms and people with brooms dusting the path. And I could see cattle and sheep roaming around outside; the smell came right into the chapel. I could see people walking on the street beyond. For heaven's sake, how can I pray in this place? The man behind me said, 'We want you to pray with your eyes wide open. That's what we do in this church.'"*

A message came wrapped in an infant's tattered blanket in a dirty manger. What do we hear, what do we smell, what is the view from where we sit? Do we pray and worship with our eyes wide open?

Mary called the baby in her womb, *My Savior*. This was a humble admission that she was a sinner and in need of salvation. She was not ashamed to say so. When we embrace the personal Gospel of salvation, the people in our lives are brought face to face with the Living God. What will the view be like from their vantage point when they look back at us? Will they see a royal Christian or a peasant Christian? Mary understood the message. Do we understand it? Pride puffs out its chest and asks: "Savior—saved from what? Saved *for* what?" All it would take for us to truly appreciate our salvation and begin taking the message of the Gospel seriously is for God to zip open the pit of hell and dangle us by our toes over the edge for a few seconds. Contrariwise, only a momentary glimpse of heaven would prove conclusively that it has all been worth it.

The story of Mary teaches us that we are eternal creatures and, as such, our lives must be lived with eternity in view. All believers should find comfort in knowing that this is not our home; we are only passing through. One of my first visits as a pastor was to the home of a very sick older gentleman whom I had never met before. He was semi-comatose and had a hard time communicating. His daughter was the organist in my first church. She told me of the lifetime of service for Christ that her dad had lived. She warned me to be careful if I picked up his Bible, because it might fall apart from years of constant use and note-taking. He had whole chapters of Scripture memorized and could direct me to any passage or verse that our topic of conversation might require. He was a true student of the Scriptures. He taught the Word for many years in Sunday school and lived it in his life. His Godly reputation was widely known.

His daughter told me this story. One night, her dad was lying on the sofa when suddenly his face brightened and he began to smile. He said, "Barbara, look!" and started naming his brothers who had passed away before him as if they were standing right in front of him. "I see them! I see them!" He then raised his hands and said, "Oh...I've been so foolish. I could have studied so much more. How little I know. How much more I could have learned!" His heart was broken because he had not spent *more* time learning the Word. He was granted a miniscule peek at what the full Glory of heaven is like. He died shortly afterwards and I am confident that, as he was ushered into the presence of his Savior, he truly realized how little he knew.

We are so earthly-minded and fixed in our own rationalism that we refuse to see that life extends beyond the temporal and that we are eternal creatures who will spend eternity somewhere, either in heaven or in hell. One million years from now, we will be alive and conscious somewhere. Satan gains a greater victory by convincing people that hell does not exist—or worse, that all men eventually go to heaven. A person meandering through life "believing in a god" while seeing no need whatsoever for a savior is the greatest victory the Evil One could hope to achieve. If there is no heaven to be gained and no hell to be shunned, then the Incarnation story becomes a meaningless fairytale and all of Scripture becomes a cruel and shameful exercise in deceit. The baby in Mary's womb was her assurance of eternal life in heaven and Mary knew it.

Continuing with verses 48 and 49:
for he has been mindful
of the humble state of his servant.
From now on all generations will call me blessed,
for the Mighty One has done great things for me –
Holy is his name.

The story of Mary teaches us that to miss the message she embraced has eternal implications. The second Stanza of her song (Luke 1:47) makes it abundantly clear that Mary recognized her need for a Savior. In this stanza, she tells us why all future generations will call her blessed. She states, *"The Mighty One has done great things for me—Holy is His name!"* She had been the one chosen, for no reason other than Grace, by the One who knew the lowly condition of her sinful heart. He was mindful of (He mapped out) the pathway to spiritual greatness, and that pathway for any Christian is to glorify the Holy One, the One who saves us.

A high-level Administration official under President Nixon was once asked why he "had not seen the light" or "gotten religion" as did certain other individuals in the White House following the Watergate break-in scandal. His joking response was, "I have not been able to find the switch." He went on to say, "I found within *myself* all I need and all I ever shall need. I am a great man of faith *but my faith is in [me]. I have never failed me."*[5] I wonder what he and others like him will say when they stand before a Holy God and He asks them, "What have you done with my Son, Jesus Christ?" Then, the pitiful response, "But Lord, I had faith in myself" will ring tragically hollow. Expounding upon our alleged great human potential and extolling our personal self-worth is an insult to the cross.

Today's moral message is, "What's right for you may be wrong for someone else." The religion of moral relativism resists any moral absolutes. "Do what feels right to you, trust yourself and it will all work out in the end." Can you imagine if young Mary had been raised that way? Christian counselors will tell you that their offices and schedules are filled with people who live by that mindset. "I'll do what I think is right and ignore the need for any moral absolutes, especially Scriptural ones."

The story of Mary teaches us to endure the ambiguities of life as we discover God's calling and purpose for us. She was not a girl living without a purpose. She knew her God and her destiny, and she marveled over the miracle within her body. *My soul glorifies the Lord and my spirit rejoices in God my Savior*. This is the intriguing story of a young peasant girl who would one day stand at the foot of a bloody cross as her heart was ripped from her chest. A holy and righteous man told Mary this would happen when she and Joseph brought their baby boy into the temple to present Him in accordance with the Law. Simeon sang another of those songs of Christmas:

"Sovereign Lord, as you have promised, you now dismiss your servant in peace. For my eyes have seen your salvation, which you have prepared in the sight of all people, a light for revelation to the Gentiles and for glory to your people Israel." The child's father and mother marveled at what was said about him. Then Simeon blessed them and said to Mary, his mother: "This child is destined to cause the falling and rising of many in Israel, and to be a sign that will be spoken

against, so that the thoughts of many hearts will be revealed. And a sword will pierce your own soul too." (Luke 2:29-35; emphasis added)

Simeon foretold the beginning and the brutal ending of Jesus' ministry on earth, and for thirty-three years she lived with that dark cloud hanging over her every waking moment. The pain would be unbearable. She was a mother. How could it be otherwise? When she watched as her baby boy was tied to a post and whipped to within an inch of His life, as she stood on Golgotha and heard the hammer striking the iron nails, as she leaned on the rough-hewn beam of the cross and felt the warmth of His blood dripping on her hands, as she listened to the provocative taunts of the crowd as they mocked the One Who loved them with an everlasting love, as she listened intently to His seven last sayings from the cross, and as she witnessed this unparalleled cruelty of man, she surely remembered Simeon's words. Memories of her little boy growing up must have flooded her soul. Watching her Son's brutal crucifixion was the sword Simeon prophesied would pierce her soul, the same soul that had so eloquently glorified God.

Mary's story did not end at the cross. One can only surmise the jubilation that came three days later when she saw her son alive and clothed in the majesty of God. If when we bury our loved ones, we can only say, "That's the end; that's all there is," then we have no message. If we have no message we have no purpose. If we have no purpose, then Paul would tell us, as he told the Corinthian church, *And if Christ has not been raised, your faith is futile; you are still in your sins* (1 Corinthians 15:17). However, we do have a message and our lives are not in vain.

~ ~ ~ ~

Harlots and Heroines—The Midwives of the Messiah! Five ordinary people were redeemed by an extraordinary Savior. We have spent some time getting to know these unique women a little better than we might have known them before. They would have remained obscure and unknown figures in the shadows of history but for being touched by the hand of God for a special purpose. For *four* of them, the tragedies and sacrifices they endured seem all the more poignant because they may never have known for certain—until Glory, when God reveals all things—what that special purpose was, and yet they persevered. Thrust into the limelight and tossed by the storms of death, poverty, war and scandal, their lives became dramatic yet necessary milestones on the long, harsh Covenant road leading from the Garden to the Manger.

Because they stood resolutely and linked hands across the generations of the Messianic genealogy, the five redeemed Faith Heroines can now rejoice in God's eternal, unstoppable plan and in the vital role that each one of them was assigned to play. As foretold, the *Seed of the Woman* entered and the head of the Serpent was dealt a crushing blow. These memorable, but wounded, women can now see clearly, and they agree—all of their fear, sorrow and heartache was well worth it.

God chose Mary in a different way than He did Tamar, Rahab, Ruth and Bathsheba. She became the fifth and final Midwife of the Messiah for good reason. It is altogether fitting that a woman of such exceptional humility and character, blameless among men, with no sordid past, should become the earthly mother of the One who would take the center stage of history—the One who was *despised and rejected by men, a man of sorrows, and familiar with suffering* (Isaiah 53:3).

Sing a song of redemption. Rejoice in God your Savior—and remember your sisters, The Midwives of the Messiah, who shared in the labor and attended the birth of the King of Kings and Lord of Lords!

---

[1] The fact of the pre-existence of Christ is confirmed many times in the New Testament (John 8:58; Philippians 2:5-11; Colossians 1:15, 16).

[2] There are a variety of names that refer to the same person, Jechoniah. He is one and the same person as Jehoiachin and Coniah.

[3] See the appendix for a further discussion of some of the complexities of the genealogy of Jesus.

---

[4] This means that Joseph should not be afraid to marry Mary. It does not mean they were living together out of wedlock.

[5] George Gordon Battle Liddy (born November 30, 1930) was the chief operative for the White House Plumbers unit that existed during several years of Richard Nixon's Presidency. Liddy masterminded the first break-in of the Democratic National Committee headquarters in the Watergate building in 1972. The subsequent cover-up of the Watergate scandal led to Nixon's resignation in 1974; Liddy served four and a half years in prison for his role in the burglary.

Appendix
The Two Genealogies of Jesus

There are two genealogies of Jesus, one in the Gospel of Matthew and the other in the Gospel of Luke. As was discussed in chapters 3 and 4, anyone who claimed to be the Messiah had to prove that he came from the tribe of Judah and that he was a blood descendant of King David. Here are some points to consider in understanding the unique purposes for which the genealogies were so meticulously recorded:

Both genealogies verify that Mary and Joseph were from the tribe of Judah.

Both genealogies verify that Jesus was a direct descendant of King David.

Matthew's account traced Jesus' lineage through His *legal* parent, Joseph, His stepfather, thus establishing Jesus' *legal* claim to be the Messiah. This line is traced back to Abraham through David's son, King Solomon.

Luke's account, on the other hand, traced Jesus' lineage through His *natural* parent, Mary, His mother. This line is traced back through David's son Nathan, thus establishing Jesus' *natural* line of descent.

This means that Jesus was *legally and naturally* an heir of King David.

One problem occurs when we learn that Joseph was a direct descendant of Jechoniah (Matthew 1:11-16). Given the Jechoniah curse (Jeremiah 22:28-30), Joseph, having the blood of Jechoniah in his veins, was not qualified to sit on David's throne. Additionally, no son of Joseph would have the right to claim the Throne of David. This is a critical point since, if Jesus were Joseph's biological son, He could not, by virtue of the curse, inherit David's throne. This is why Matthew goes on to show that Jesus was not Joseph's biological son, for He was born of the virgin, Mary (Matthew 1:18-25).

Luke's genealogy traces the line of Mary back to King David (Luke 3:31-32). A careful reading of Luke's genealogy will show that the son of David referred to is not Solomon but Nathan. Thus, in Luke's genealogy it is demonstrated that Mary came from the tribe of Judah (a requirement for whomever claimed to be the Messiah), and was a member of the House of David totally apart from the curse of Jechoniah. Because of His mother's lineage, Jesus was also a member of the House of David, totally apart from the curse of Jechoniah. This is how Jesus fulfilled two of the Old Testament requirements for kingship.

Another problem occurs in Luke 3:23 where it states, *Now Jesus himself was about thirty years old when he began his ministry. He was the son, so it was thought, of Joseph, the son of Heli.* However, in Matthew's genealogy, Joseph's father is called Jacob and not Heli (Matthew 1:16). Although Mary's name is not mentioned in Luke's genealogy, we know that this account is her genealogy given the fact that Heli was not Joseph's father. This means that Heli was Mary's father, making Joseph his son-in-law. The reason Mary is not mentioned is that women rarely were listed in one's genealogy. This is what makes the five Midwives of the Messiah in Matthew's account so unusual.

Thus, Jesus had the genealogical credentials of being a son of Abraham, Judah, and David, by both legal right through his stepfather, Joseph, and by natural descent through Mary.

About the Author

Dr. Chuck Betters, an ordained pastor since 1969, has served in a variety of cultural settings including the inner city during the seventies. Chuck likes to say he cut his teeth in ministry on the streets of Philadelphia. For his entire career he has focused on not only the "thus says the Lord" aspects of Scripture but also the "so what" of Scripture–the practical exercise of Biblical truth. Chuck's uncompromising style has led thousands over the years to appreciate his holistic approach to Biblical preaching and teaching–what Chuck likes to call the "blue denim and lace" balance between the truth (logos) of the Scriptures, its ethical demands (ethos), and the great passion (pathos) with which he presents it.

Chuck and his wife, Sharon, have been married since 1969. They have four children. Their youngest son, Mark, was safely deposited in heaven when he was killed in a car accident in 1993. Chuck says of this tragedy that, "God, in His sovereignty, scorched my life in such a way that He unbolted me from my love affair with this world." Their two older sons, Chuck and Dan, serve in full-time pastoral ministry on the staff where Chuck is the Senior Pastor of the Glasgow Reformed Presbyterian Church (PCA) in Glasgow, Delaware. Their only daughter, Heidi, is a mother to five children and serves as the event coordinator for MARKINC Ministries, the media arm of Chuck's preaching and teaching ministry. Chuck and Sharon have 14 grandchildren.

Chuck is the author of *Teaching Them Young: The Hidden Treasures of the Proverbs.*

Visit **www.markinc.org** *to order these products and download hundreds of FREE messages and articles!*

Books

Treasures in Darkness:
A Grieving Mother Shares Her Heart
Sharon W. Betters

Treasures of Encouragement:
Women Helping Women
in the Church
Sharon W. Betters

Treasures of Faith:
Living Boldly in View of
God's Promises
Chuck and Sharon Betters

Treasures of Faith:
Living Boldly in View of
God's Promises—
A Leader's Guide
Chuck and Sharon Betters

Teaching Them Young:
The Hidden Treasures of the Proverbs
Chuck Betters

Teaching Them Young:
The Hidden Treasures of the
Proverbs
Chuck Betters

More inspirational resources from MARKINC Ministries…

CDs

Learning to See When the Lights Go Out series

Alcoholism: Hope and Help

Dying with Dignity and Grace

Autism Spectrum Disorders: Speaking Hope

First Responders: Wounded Healers

Terminal Illness

Coming Home from War series

Loss of a Loved One

Breast Cancer

Adultery: Forgiveness and Redemption

MARKINC Ministries is committed to leaning into the pain of life experiences that often go unnoticed by the church. The ***Learning to See When the Lights Go Out*** CD series addresses many of life's darkest circumstances that are often difficult to discuss, and shows us how we can help our fellow Christians continue to walk by faith even when darkness falls. These CDs contain the real-life testimonies of men and women who have walked through painful experiences and, by God's grace, ultimately learned how to see *when the lights went out.*

Visit **www.markinc.org** *to order these products and download hundreds of FREE messages and articles!*

Breinigsville, PA USA
12 November 2009

227458BV00002B/2/P